THE CHICKEN SMELLS GOOD

2 Edition

Dialogs & Stories

WILLIAM P. PICKETT

Passaic High School

Longman

Pickett, William P.
     The chicken smells good : dialogs & stories / William P. Pickett.
 -- 2nd ed.
       p. cm.
    Includes index.
    ISBN 0-13-576216-2
    1. English language--Textbooks for foreign speakers.   I. Title.
PE1128.P482   1997
428.6' 4—DC21   96-37552
                                                             CIP

Publisher: *Mary Jane Peluso*
Editor: *Sheryl Olinsky*
Development Editor: *Gino Mastascusa*
Electronic Production Editor: *Paula D. Williams*
Manufacturing Manager: *Ray Keating*

Art Director: *Merle Krumper*
Interior Design: *Paula D. Williams, Wanda España*
Cover Design: *Susan Newman Design, Inc.*
Illustrations: *Don Martinetti*

© 1997 by PRENTICE HALL REGENTS

A Pearson Education Company
Pearson Education, 10 Bank Street, White Plains, NY 10606

Printed in the United States of America

10   9   8   7   6   5

ISBN   0-13-576216-2

To My Wife, Dorothy

Contents

PREFACE viii

 LOVE AND MARRIAGE 1

Going to Lunch   2

I Love to Dance   6

I'm Crazy About You   10

Madly in Love   14

Promises, Promises   18

 FOOD AND WORK 23

It's Easy to Open a Can of Spaghetti   24

The Chicken Smells Good   28

All Bosses Are Demanding   32

Ice Cream, Candy, and Potato Chips   36

Pete Loves Sports and Gambling   40

ACHES AND PAINS   45

Heart Trouble Is Always Serious   46

Put On Plenty of BENGAY   50

A Pain in the Side   54

    A Busy Manager   58

    A Hug and a Kiss   62

FAMILIES AND PETS   67

A Brown Puppy   68

A Famous Cherry Tree   72

Kids Are Different Today   76

    Three Children, a Dog, and a Cat   80

    Mark and Carol   84

ENGLISH AND JOBS   89

English Is a Crazy Language   90

Where Do You Want to Go, Ma'am?   94

A Tough Teacher   98

    Looking for a Job   102

    Good Tips and High Hopes   106

COUPLES AND HOUSING 111

No Kiss This Morning?   112

A Mouse in the Kitchen   116

It's a Deal   120

    The Roaches Are Back   124

    A Bargain and a Bribe   128

CARS AND TRAVEL   133

I Want to Learn to Drive   134

Our Car Is Falling Apart   138

Canada or Mexico   142

    Wild Bill   146

    Lucky to be Alive   150

WOMEN AND DECISIONS 155

A Siren and Flashing Lights   156

Are You Deaf, Lady?   160

The Old Approach   164

    The Extra Money Would Help   168

    A Tough Decision   172

Word List   177

Preface

OVERVIEW

The Chicken Smells Good is a reader whose dialogs and stories tell of the problems and progress and the strengths and weaknesses of ordinary people. Its twenty-four dialogs and sixteen stories are written to entertain, inform, touch emotions, and lead to student comment. They include a variety of themes, settings, and characters.

The best way to get students to read and to improve their reading skills is to make reading interesting and enjoyable, and that is the aim of this book.

The Chicken is written in a colloquial style, and its vocabulary and grammar are informal. The book is also realistic, and its characters have faults and shortcomings as well as virtues.

NEW FEATURES IN THE SECOND EDITION

The second edition of *The Chicken* features three new dialogs ("A Brown Puppy," "A Tough Teacher," and "Canada or Mexico"), a glossary (Word Preview) and preview questions before all dialogs and stories, dialog reviews, and cloze and matching exercises.

The dialog about the boxers Muhammad Ali and Joe Louis in the first edition of *The Chicken* has been replaced because fewer and fewer students know about Ali or Louis. Small but important changes have been made in the other dialogs and stories. Unnecessary words have been omitted, salaries and prices have been adjusted for inflation, and some lines and sentences have been modified or dropped to make the dialogs and stories clearer or more interesting.

Most of the true-false questions have been replaced with factual, opinion, or inference questions.

The Answer Key has been placed in a separate booklet, and an audio tape has been added.

LEVEL

The Chicken is intended for advanced beginners or low-intermediate students. It presupposes that its readers already know the most basic vocabulary and structures of English. At the same time, it avoids advanced vocabulary and complicated structures.

OBJECTIVES

The Chicken Smells Good aims to

- Improve reading skills
- Expand vocabulary
- Increase fluency through role-playing and discussion
- Improve listening comprehension

AUDIENCE

The Chicken is written for young adults and adults of all ages.   It is intended for college, community-college, and high-school students, as well as adult-education classes and students who are studying on their own.

CONTENTS

A. Word Preview

Every dialog and story is preceded by a Word Preview section that defines all the key words used in the dialog or story and gives an example sentence for each key word. This section is a glossary and not a dictionary, so with few exceptions, its definitions include only the way the words are used in the dialog or story.

Some teachers may wish to use the Word Preview section *after* reading the dialog or story. Teachers can experiment and decide whether it's best for them to use this section before or after the dialogs and stories.

For many of the key words, two definitions are given in the Word Preview. When these definitions are basically the same, a *semi-colon* is used to separate them. When they are different, a *colon* is used to separate them.

B. Preview Questions

Preview questions introduce all dialogs and stories.   The purpose of these questions is to stimulate a student's prior knowledge of and interest in the topic of the dialog or story.

C. Dialog or Story

Three dialogs and two stories are the heart of each of the eight chapters of *The Chicken*.   The dialogs are meant to be listened to, read, and role-played, but not memorized.   The stories are to be listened to and read.

D. Comprehension Questions

Comprehension questions follow the dialogs and stories.   Students must use their own ideas to answer questions with an asterisk.   Sometimes the comprehension questions are true-false questions.

E. Dialog Review

In addition to comprehension questions, all of the dialogs are followed by a Dialog Review section.   This section repeats the ideas of the dialog in non-dialog form and tests and reinforces a student's vocabulary.

F. Sharing Information

All dialogs and stories are followed by a Sharing Information section. This section gives students an opportunity to express their own ideas and opinions.   It fosters a more independent use of English and aims to improve the students' fluency.

G. Story Completion and Matching

Every chapter contains three story-completion exercises and a word-matching exercise.   These exercises review and reinforce the vocabulary used in the dialogs and stories.

H. Synonyms and Antonyms

Every chapter concludes with a synonym and an antonym exercise. These exercises also review and reinforce some of the more important words used in the chapter.

I. Word List

A word list, containing all of the words defined in the Word Preview section, is provided in the back of the book.

REVIEW TESTS, ANSWER KEY, AND AUDIO CASSETTE

Vocabulary review tests for all eight chapters of *The Chicken* and an Answer Key for both the book and the review tests have been placed in a separate booklet.

An audio cassette of *The Chicken* is also available so that students can listen to the dialogs and stories of this book in the classroom, in the language lab, in their car, and in their home.

THE CHICKEN SMELLS GOOD AND THE PIZZA TASTES GREAT

The Pizza Tastes Great is a reader written in a style and format similar to *The Chicken Smells Good*. However, *The Pizza* is a much easier book. Its dialogs and stories are shorter, its vocabulary and structures more controlled, and its exercises less difficult.

Acknowledgements

I wish to thank everyone at Prentice Hall Regents who helped in the publishing of the Second Edition of *The Chicken*. I am particularly grateful to Sheryl Olinsky and Nancy Baxer, my editors, to Gino Mastascusa, my development editor, and to Paula D. Williams, my production editor. All were most helpful and made important contributions to this book.

I also wish to thank Don Martinetti who did the art work for *The Chicken* and who took great pains to capture the spirit and details of its dialogs and stories.

Above all, I am grateful to my wife, Dorothy, for her careful reading of all the drafts of this book and for her many helpful suggestions.

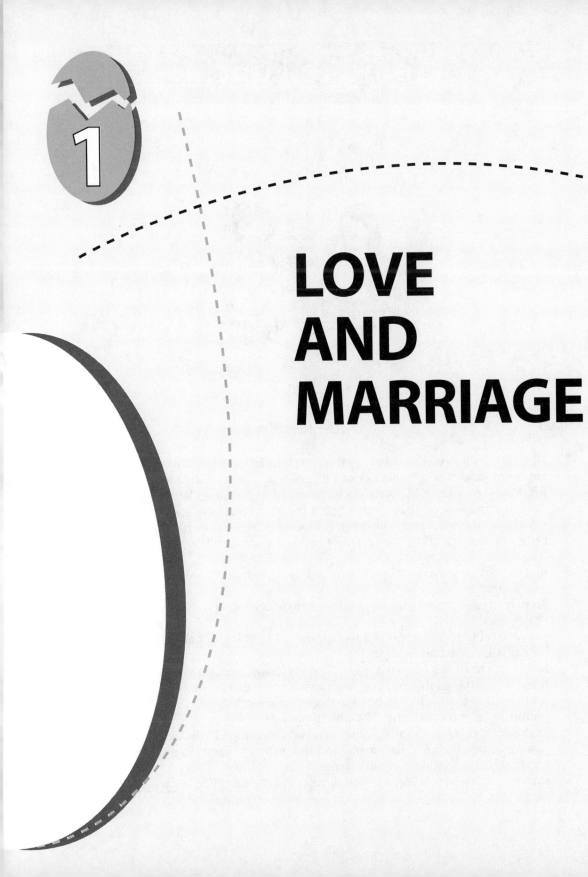

1

LOVE
AND
MARRIAGE

Going to Lunch

1. **a lot of** *idiom* much; many "A thousand dollars is <u>a lot of</u> money."
2. **anymore** *adv.* now "Janet doesn't live here <u>anymore</u>. She moved to Florida."
3. **Big Mac**® *n.* a large McDonald's hamburger with cheese, lettuce, pickles, onions, and sauce "Pat always gets a <u>Big Mac</u> when she goes to McDonald's."
4. **calorie** *n.* the amount of energy in a food "A large apple has about 90 <u>calories</u>."
5. **certainly** *adv.* clearly "We <u>certainly</u> need more money if we're going to buy a car."
6. **diet** *n.* a plan to eat less food "Sam is having fish and a salad for dinner. He's on a <u>diet</u>."
7. **French fries** *n.* thin strips of potatoes cooked in deep fat "These <u>French fries</u> taste good."
8. **get** *v.* to obtain: to obtain at a restaurant "I'm going to <u>get</u> spaghetti and meatballs. What are you <u>getting</u>?"
9. **lose** *v.* to have less of something "Fred is <u>losing</u> his hair."
10. **luck** *n.* the things that happen to a person by chance, especially the good things "Alice likes to play bingo, but she doesn't have much <u>luck</u>."
11. **pound** *n.* a unit of weight "I want 10 <u>pounds</u> of sugar."
12. **shake** *n.* a drink with milk, ice cream, and flavoring (To make a *shake*, you shake or mix the milk, ice cream, and flavoring.) "Cindy is getting an orange soda, and I'm getting a vanilla <u>shake</u>."
13. **starve** *v.* to be very hungry "Joe didn't eat breakfast. He's <u>starving</u>."

PREVIEW QUESTIONS

Discuss these questions before reading the dialog.

1. What do you usually eat for lunch? And drink for lunch?
2. Do you usually eat lunch with someone? If so, who do you eat with?
3. Do you like to eat at McDonald's or Burger King? If so, why? Do you eat there often?

Maria and Pedro are computer programmers. They work for the telephone company and are very good friends. They often eat lunch together. Maria is on a diet. She loves hamburgers and French fries, but she can't have them on her diet.

Pedro: What time is it?

Maria: It's twelve o'clock.

Pedro: I'm starving.

Maria: Me too![1]

Pedro: I'm going to lunch.

Maria: Where are you going?

Pedro: To McDonald's.

Maria: Good. I'm going with you.

Pedro: What are you having?

Maria: A salad and coffee.

Pedro: No hamburger and French fries?

Maria: Not anymore.

Pedro: Why not? You like them.

Maria: Yes, but they have a lot of calories.

Pedro: Are you on a diet?

Maria: Yes, I want to lose 20 pounds.

Pedro: Good luck!

Maria: Thanks. What are you getting?

Pedro: A Big Mac, French fries, and a chocolate shake.

Maria: Well, *you're* certainly not on a diet!

---

1. **Me too** is a short way of saying *I am too*, or *I do too*. It is informal and correct English.

COMPREHENSION

Answer these questions in pairs or small groups. Use your own ideas to answer questions with an asterisk. (* = asterisk)

1. What time is Pedro going to lunch?
*2. Why do you think he likes to go to McDonald's for lunch?
3. What is Maria having for lunch?
4. Why isn't she getting a hamburger and French fries?
5. How many pounds does she want to lose?
6. What is Pedro getting for lunch?
*7. Do you think that McDonald's is a good place to eat if you're on a diet? Explain your answer.

DIALOG REVIEW

Complete the paragraphs with these words.

lose	**French fries**	**shake**	**diet**	**starving**
a lot of	**certainly**	**luck**	**anymore**	**getting**

It's twelve o'clock, and Pedro and Maria are going to lunch. They're

_____ .

Maria is having a salad and coffee. Pedro wants to know why she isn't

having a hamburger and _____ . She says she's not having

them _____ because they have _____

calories.

Pedro asks Maria if she's on a _____ . She tells him

she is and that she wants to _____ 20 pounds.

He wishes her _____ .

Pedro is _____ a Big Mac, French fries, and a

chocolate _____ . Maria says he's _____

not on a diet.

SHARING INFORMATION

Discuss these questions in pairs or small groups.

1. Why do children like to eat at McDonald's?
2. Do you like hamburgers?
3. Do you like French fries?
4. Name some of your favorite foods.
5. What is your favorite drink?
6. Do you like shakes?
7. Name some foods that have a lot of calories.
8. Name some foods that don't have very many calories.
9. Maria and Pedro are computer programmers. Do you think that's a good job? Explain your answer.
10. Do you like to work with computers? Why or why not?

DICTATION

1. *Listen while the teacher reads the dialog without stopping.* <u>*Don't write anything*</u>.

2. *The teacher will read the dialog a second time, pausing after the missing lines.* <u>*Write in the missing lines*</u>.

3. *The teacher will read the dialog a third time.* <u>*Check your work*</u>.

Pedro: I'm going to lunch.

Maria: _____

Pedro: To McDonald's.

Maria: _____

Pedro: What are you having?

Maria: _____

Pedro: No hamburger and French fries?

Maria: _____

Pedro: Why not? You like them.

Maria: _____

I Love to Dance

1. **ago** *adv.* in the past "Leonid came to the United States from Russia a year <u>ago</u>."
2. **around** *adv.* close to "The watch costs <u>around</u> $90."
3. **break** *n.* rest from work "I'm tired. Let's take a <u>break</u>."
4. **especially** *adv.* to a special degree; more than others "Stephanie likes sports, <u>especially</u> tennis."
5. **feeling** *n.* what a person feels, for example, happiness or love "It's a great <u>feeling</u> to be home from the hospital."
6. **go shopping** *v.* to go to one or more stores to buy something "My wife and I like to <u>go shopping</u> at the mall."
7. **have to** *idiom* must; be necessary "I <u>have to</u> go to the post office. I need stamps." (*Have to* changes to *has to* when the subject is *he, she,* or *it.*)
8. **keep** *v.* to continue: to cause to continue "<u>Keep</u> practicing the guitar and you'll get better." "We need a police officer to <u>keep</u> the traffic moving."
9. **merengue** *n.* a popular Latin dance, especially popular in the Dominican Republic "Rosa likes to dance the <u>merengue</u>."
10. **pick up** *v.* to go in a car to get someone "Ahmed will <u>pick up</u> Raja at the airport."
11. **special** *adj.* not ordinary "Tomorrow is a <u>special</u> day. It's my 21st birthday."
12. **sure** *adv.* certainly; yes "Are you and Alan going to the party?" "<u>Sure</u>, we love parties."
13. **too** *adv.* more than is good or necessary "I can't wear these pants. They're <u>too</u> big."
14. **worry** *v.* to be anxious "My grandmother lives alone. I <u>worry</u> about her."

PREVIEW QUESTIONS

Discuss these questions before reading the dialog.

1. What do you usually do on Saturdays?
2. Do you like to dance?
3. Do you have a favorite dance? What is it?

Maria is from the Dominican Republic, and Pedro is from Colombia. They're single, and they like to go out together.   They meet on the elevator on their way to work and are talking. Maria loves to dance. So does Pedro. It's Friday, and they're both tired.

Pedro:　Thank God it's Friday![1]

Maria:　Yes, it sure is a nice feeling.

Pedro:　What are you doing tomorrow?

Maria:　In the morning I have to go shopping. And you?

Pedro:　Nothing special. I'm going to sleep late.

Maria:　You're lucky.

Pedro:　Would you like[2] to go to a dance with me?

Maria:　Sure. I love to dance, especially the merengue.

Pedro:　Great! I'll pick you up at your house.

Maria:　At what time?

Pedro:　Around eight. Please don't keep me waiting.

Maria:　What are you talking about? I never keep you waiting.

Pedro:　What about two weeks ago? I waited an hour for you!

Maria:　Oh, that's right. Well, I won't be late tomorrow.

Pedro:　I hope not.

Maria:　See you at the coffee break.

Pedro:　OK. Don't work too hard.

Maria:　Don't worry. I won't.

1. Pedro **thanks God it's Friday** because he doesn't have to work on Saturday or Sunday. *Thank God it's Friday!* is a common saying.
2. **Would you like** is an idiom that means *to offer* or *to invite*. "Would you like a cold drink?" "Would you like to go to the movies?"

TRUE OR FALSE

If the sentence is true, write T. *If it's false, write* F.

_____   1. Maria and Pedro like the weekends.

_____   2. Maria has nothing to do on Saturday morning.

_____   3. Pedro is going to sleep late on Saturday.

_____   4. The merengue is Maria's favorite dance.

_____   5. Pedro is going to meet her at the dance.

_____   6. Maria was late for a date two weeks ago.

_____   7. Pedro wants her to work harder.

_____   8. She won't see him until lunch time.

DIALOG REVIEW

Complete the paragraphs with these words.

would	around	worry	feeling	ago
too	has to	keep	pick up	special

Pedro thanks God that it's Friday, and Maria agrees that it's a nice _____ .   She _____ go shopping tomorrow morning, but Pedro has nothing _____ to do, so he's going to sleep late. He's lucky.

Pedro asks Maria if she _____ like to go to a dance with him. She says yes. She loves to dance, especially the merengue.

He is going to _____ Maria at her house _____ eight. He asks her not to _____ him waiting. He waited an hour for her two weeks _____ .

Pedro tells Maria not to work _____ hard. She tells him not to _____ . She won't.

SHARING INFORMATION

Discuss these questions in pairs or small groups.

1. Do you usually sleep late on Saturdays?
2. Name a dance that is especially popular in your country.
3. Do you dance much?
4. Where do you go to dance?
5. Are you a good dancer?
6. Do you usually get to school, parties, and appointments on time?
7. When is it important to be on time? Why?
8. When isn't it so important to be on time? Why?
9. In general, do people in the United States place a lot of importance to being on time?
10. Is being on time as important in your country?

STORY COMPLETION

An Important Test

Dianne is studying for an important math test that she has tomorrow. She's tired, but she decides not to stop studying.

Complete the story with these words.

would	**ago**	**around**	**worries**
keep	**has to**	**break**	**especially**

Dianne is tired, but she _____ study tonight because she has an important math test tomorrow.

It's _____ 9:30, and Dianne _____ like to take a _____ , but she decides to _____ studying.

She _____ a lot before tests, _____ math tests. Two weeks _____ , she did poorly on a math test.

I'm Crazy About You

1. **absolutely** *adv.* completely "You're absolutely right."
2. **crazy about** *idiom* love very much: have a great interest in "Ed is crazy about Laura." "Mark is crazy about soccer."
3. **darling** *n.* a person who is loved very much (We often address those we love very much as *darling, dear, honey,* or *love.*) "I'm going, darling. I'll be home around five."
4. **explain** *v.* to give reasons for "The governor is explaining why we need a tax increase."
5. **forever** *adv.* never coming to an end "This bad weather can't continue forever."
6. **just** *adv.* only "Sarah isn't sick. She's just tired."
7. **kind** *adj.* friendly; ready to help others "Joshua will help you. He's very kind."
8. **of course** *idiom* naturally; certainly "Of course, it's important to have friends."
9. **silly** *adj.* foolish; stupid "It's silly to keep a lot of money in your wallet."
10. **so** *adv.* very "Caroline has a new job. She's so happy."
11. **step** *n.* an action followed by other actions "If you want to become a lawyer, the first step is to go to college."
12. **such** *adv.* very "We learn a lot in Mrs. Kim's class. She's such a good teacher."
13. **wonderful** *adj.* very good "We had a wonderful vacation."

PREVIEW QUESTIONS

Discuss these questions before reading the dialog.

1. Explain what love is by completing this sentence. Love is _____

_____.

2. Is it easy for people to explain why they love someone?
3. Love is necessary for a successful marriage. What else is important?

Maria and Pedro are in love. Pedro is 25 years old, and Maria is 23. He wants to marry Maria. She also wants to marry him, but she has to be sure before she says yes.

Maria:	I love you, Pedro!
Pedro:	I love you too, darling!
Maria:	How much do you love me?
Pedro:	A lot. I'm crazy about you!
Maria:	Why do you love me so much?
Pedro:	You're kind, you're pretty. You understand me.
Maria:	Don't stop! Tell me more!
Pedro:	I . . . I can't explain it. I just love you.
Maria:	And I love you more than anyone in the world.
Pedro:	Can I ask you a question?
Maria:	Sure.
Pedro:	Will you marry me?
Maria:	Marriage is such a big step, honey.
Pedro:	I know, but we're in love. That's all we need.
Maria:	Will you love me forever?
Pedro:	Of course, silly.
Maria:	Are you absolutely sure?
Pedro:	Yes, yes! Absolutely!
Maria:	Wonderful! Let's[1] get married in June!

---

1. **Let's** = let us.   *Let's* is used to make a suggestion.   "We're hungry. Let's eat." = "I suggest that we eat since we're hungry."

COMPREHENSION

Answer these questions in pairs or small groups. Use your own ideas to answer questions with an asterisk.

1. How much does Pedro love Maria?
2. Why does he love her?
*3. Do you think she is surprised by Pedro's marriage proposal? Explain your answer.
4. Why is she slow to say yes to his proposal?
5. What does he say is the only thing necessary for their marriage?
*6. Why isn't Maria upset when he calls her silly?
*7. Why do you think she wants to get married in June?

DIALOG REVIEW

Complete the paragraphs with these words.

explain	such	kind	wonderful	forever
step	crazy about	of course	just	so

Pedro loves Maria a lot. He's _____ her. She asks him why he loves her _____ much.   Pedro says it's because she's _____ and pretty and understands him. Maria asks for more reasons, but he says he can't _____ it. He _____ loves her, and she loves him more than anyone in the world.

Pedro asks Maria to marry him.   She replies that marriage is _____ a big _____. He says he knows that, but they're in love, and that's all they need.

Maria asks Pedro if he will love her _____ . He says _____ he will. She wants to know if he's absolutely sure. He says he is, and she says that's _____ and suggests that they get married in June.

SHARING INFORMATION

Discuss these questions in pairs or small groups.

1. Why do we use the word *crazy* to describe those who are in love?
2. Maria and Pedro are both interested in computers. Is it important for married couples to have common interests? Explain your answer.
3. Do you think that rich people have happier marriages than those who don't have much money? Explain your answer.
4. Can a couple be absolutely sure their love will last forever? Explain your answer.
5. How old do you think a woman should be before she considers marriage? How old should a man be?
6. Is it important that a married couple be about the same age? Explain your answer.
7. What is the most popular month for weddings in your country?
8. What are some wedding customs in the United States?
9. Are weddings in your country the same as in the United States? Name any differences you can think of.
10. Are expressions of love, like *darling* and *honey*, common in your country?

MATCHING

Match the words in Column A with their definitions or descriptions in Column B. Print the letters on the blank lines.

Column A		Column B	
__H__	1. ago	A.	what we do at malls
_____	2. luck	B.	a plan to eat less
_____	3. keep	C.	foolish
_____	4. diet	D.	a rest period
_____	5. forever	E.	what one needs to win the lottery
_____	6. silly	F.	very
_____	7. merengue	G.	to have less of
_____	8. so	H.	in the past
_____	9. go shopping	I.	certainly
_____	10. break	J.	without end
_____	11. lose	K.	to continue
_____	12. sure	L.	a Latin dance

Madly in Love

WORD PREVIEW

1. **attractive** *adj.* pretty   "Carmen is very <u>attractive</u>."
2. **besides** *adv.* in addition   "Kyle isn't going to play golf today. He doesn't feel well. <u>Besides</u>, it may rain."
3. **bowling** *n.* a game in which each player tries to knock down ten pins with a heavy ball.   "My wife and I go <u>bowling</u> every Friday night."
4. **bright** *adj.* intelligent; smart   "Amy does very well in school. She's <u>bright</u>."
5. **couple** *n.* a man and woman who are married or considering marriage   "Curtis and Paula are a nice <u>couple</u>."
6. **favorite** *n.* someone or something that is liked the most   "I like all my teachers, but Mr. Shah is my <u>favorite</u>."
7. **handsome** *adj.* good-looking (used especially of men)   "There are many <u>handsome</u> actors in Hollywood."
8. **hesitate** *v.* to be slow or unwilling to act   "Don't <u>hesitate</u> to tell me what you think."
9. **however** *conj.* but   "That suit is expensive. <u>However</u>, I'm going to buy it."
10. **madly in love** *idiom* to love very much   "Jennifer and Brian are <u>madly in love</u>."
11. **only** *adj.* and no others   "It's the <u>only</u> hotel in the city."
12. **own** *adj.* belonging to oneself   "Mohammed has his <u>own</u> computer."
13. **seem** *v.* to appear to be   "Melissa and Sharon <u>seem</u> to be good friends."
14. **shy** *adj.* timid; fearful   "George doesn't say much. He's <u>shy</u>."
15. **so** *adv.* also; too   "Ellen is a nurse, and <u>so</u> is her sister."
16. **social worker** *n.* a person who helps others with their problems   "A <u>social worker</u> got Wayne into a program to help him stop using drugs."
17. **together** *adv.* with one another   "Regina and I are in the same class, and we often study <u>together</u>."

PREVIEW QUESTIONS

Discuss these questions before reading the story.

1. How many brothers and sisters do you have?
2. What does a social worker do?
3. How does a couple know that they're in love?

Kathy is a nurse at the Los Angeles County Medical Center. She's attractive and very bright. Yesterday she celebrated her 24th birthday. There are five children in her family. She's the youngest and the only girl. She's her father's favorite.

Kathy is madly in love with Bob. He's tall and handsome, and he's two years older than Kathy. Bob is a social worker and is good at helping people with their problems. He's a little shy, but he's very friendly when he knows you. He's an only child, and he's crazy about Kathy.

Bob and Kathy spend a lot of time together. He takes her out to dinner every Saturday night. She loves to eat out. Besides, she's always happy when she's with Bob. After dinner, they go dancing.

Kathy lives at home with her parents, but Bob has his own apartment. On Sunday afternoon, she goes to his apartment. He usually cooks dinner. He's an excellent cook, and so is Kathy. After dinner, they frequently go to a movie or watch a video on his VCR. Sometimes they go bowling.

Bob and Kathy seem to be a perfect couple. He wants to marry her, and she wants to marry him. However, one thing makes her hesitate. Bob drinks too much!

TRUE OR FALSE

If the sentence is true, write T. *If it's false, write* F.

_____ 1. Kathy is smart.

_____ 2. She has four brothers.

_____ 3. Bob comes from a large family.

_____ 4. Kathy has her own apartment.

_____ 5. She likes to eat in restaurants.

_____ 6. Bob is a businessman.

_____ 7. He and Kathy like movies and bowling.

_____ 8. Bob has a problem which Kathy isn't happy about.

STORY COMPLETION

A Bank Teller

Lindsay works in a bank. She loves her job, but she may not go to work today. She's very tired, and it's snowing hard.

Complete the story with these words.

seems	however	shy	only
besides	together	own	hesitates

Lindsay is a bank teller and drives to work every day. She has her _____ car.

Lindsay likes her job a lot. _____ , she's not going to work today. She's very tired. _____ , it's snowing hard, and she _____ to drive in the snow.

Lindsay is very _____ , and she doesn't have many friends. Allison, who also works at the bank, _____ to be her _____ good friend. Lindsay and Allison like to eat lunch and to shop _____ .

SHARING INFORMATION

Discuss these questions in pairs or small groups. Space is provided to write your answers if you wish.

1. Would you like to be a social worker? Explain your answer.

   _____

   _____

2. How much education does a person need to be a social worker?

   _____

   _____

3. Kathy is a nurse, and Bob is a social worker. What do their jobs have in common?

   _____

   _____

4. Do you like to eat in restaurants? If so, why?

   _____

   _____

5. Why don't people eat more often in restaurants?

   _____

   _____

6. How often do you go to the movies?

   _____

   _____

7. How often do you watch a movie on a VCR?

   _____

   _____

8. Do you ever go bowling? If so, how often and who do you bowl with?

   _____

   _____

Promises, Promises

WORD PREVIEW

1. **as soon as** *conj.* when "We're going to watch TV <u>as soon as</u> we finish eating."
2. **believe** *v.* to think something is true "I <u>believe</u> Larry went to New York."
3. **diamond** *n.* a very hard, valuable stone used in making rings and other jewelry "<u>Diamond</u> rings are very expensive."
4. **disappear** *v.* to be seen no more: to exist no more "Terry can't find her ring. It <u>disappeared</u>." "My headache <u>disappeared</u>."
5. **drunk** *adj.* having had too much alcohol to drink "Vince had too much beer at our party and got <u>drunk</u>."
6. **engagement** *n.* a formal promise to marry "Donna and Gary announced their <u>engagement</u>. They're going to get married in May."
7. **foolish** *adj.* stupid "You were <u>foolish</u> to fight with your boss."
8. **from time to time** *idiom* sometimes; on occasion "I see Matt <u>from time to time</u>."
9. **lonely** *adj.* unhappy because of a feeling of being alone "Stacy's husband is in the hospital, and she's <u>lonely</u>."
10. **old-fashioned** *adj.* think and act as people did in the past "My parents are <u>old-fashioned</u>."
11. **promise** *v.* to say that you will do something "Ken <u>promised</u> to clean his room."
12. **react** *v.* to act in reply to something; to respond "The doctor <u>reacted</u> quickly to the call for help."
13. **set** *adj.* arranged; ready "Everything for the picnic is <u>set</u>."
14. **situation** *n.* the way things are "Paul isn't working and doesn't have enough money to pay his bills. It's a serious <u>situation</u>."
15. **trust** *v.* to feel that someone is honest and wants to help "Angela is my best friend. I <u>trust</u> her."
16. **view** *n.* an idea; an opinion "My brother and I have different <u>views</u> on politics."
17. **warn** *v.* to say that something is dangerous or difficult "The teacher <u>warned</u> us that the test would be long and hard."
18. **wonder** *v.* to want to know; to ask oneself "I <u>wonder</u> where I put my watch."

PREVIEW QUESTIONS

Discuss these questions before reading the story.

1. An alcoholic is a person who drinks too much and cannot control his or her drinking. Do you think that a person who likes to drink and occasionally gets drunk is an alcoholic? Explain your answer.
2. Do you think it's foolish to marry an alcoholic? Explain your answer.
3. If your brother or sister were madly in love with an alcoholic and wanted to marry him or her, what would you say?

After work on Friday, Bob goes to his favorite bar. He has a few drinks with some friends from work and then goes home. When he gets home, he continues to drink. He loves Scotch,[1] and he often gets drunk on Friday night. Bob cannot control his drinking.

Kathy and Bob discuss his problem from time to time, and he promises to stop drinking as soon as they're married. Kathy believes he will keep his promise.

She thinks Bob drinks too much because he's lonely. When they're married, he won't be lonely anymore. "His drinking problem will disappear," she says. "He needs the love and attention of a wife. Marriage will change him."

Kathy's parents are very unhappy about the situation. They warn her not to marry Bob. "You're foolish to marry a man who drinks too much," they tell her.

"You don't understand how much I love Bob and how much he loves me," she replies. "Your views on love and marriage are old-fashioned." She trusts Bob. She won't listen to her parents.

Yesterday was Kathy's birthday. Bob gave her a diamond engagement ring.[2] The date for the wedding is set. Tonight she's going to show the ring to her parents. She wonders how they'll react and what they'll say.

---

1. **Scotch** is a type of whiskey made in Scotland. (Whiskey is a strong alcoholic drink.) "Before dinner, Dan had a Scotch, and I had a glass of wine."
2. In the United States, when a couple make a formal promise to marry, the man gives a ring to the woman—usually a **diamond ring**.

COMPREHENSION

Answer these questions in pairs or small groups. Use your own ideas to answer questions with an asterisk.

1.   What does Bob do after work on Friday?
*2.   Do you think he's an alcoholic? Explain your answer.
3.   What does he promise to do as soon as he's married?
*4.   Do you think he'll keep his promise? Explain your answer.
5.   What does Kathy think is the cause of Bob's drinking?
*6.   Do you think her love for Bob makes it difficult for her to think clearly about his problem? Explain your answer.
7.   What warning do Kathy's parents give her?
8.   What did Bob give her yesterday?

STORY COMPLETION

Young But Not Modern

Miss Esposito is Jerry's teacher.   She's only 26 years old, but she's not modern.   She doesn't give her students the opportunity to express themselves. However, she's young and that may change.

wonder	**warns**	**set**	**old-fashioned**
foolish	**believe**	**as soon as**	**views**

My name is Jerry, and Miss Esposito is my science teacher.   I like Miss Esposito, and I _____ she's a good teacher.   She makes her classes interesting, but she's also very _____.

I _____ why. She's only 26 years old.

_____ the bell rings, Miss Esposito collects our homework. Then she _____ us not to talk.

Miss   Esposito   never   gives   us   a   chance   to   express   our _____.   I think that's _____, but she may change. She's too young to be so _____ in her ways.

SHARING INFORMATION

Discuss these questions in pairs or small groups. Space is provided to write your answers if you wish.

1. Alcoholics Anonymous is a group that helps alcoholics with their drinking problem. What do you know about this group?

    _____

    _____

2. Alcoholics frequently deny that they have a drinking problem. Why does this keep them from solving their problem?

    _____

    _____

3. How does a person feel the day after he or she had too much to drink?

    _____

    _____

4. It's very dangerous to drink and drive, and sometimes drunk drivers kill people. Do you think that a drunk driver who kills someone should be put in jail? If so, for how long? Explain your answer.

    _____

    _____

5. Does marriage change people? Explain your answer.

    _____

    _____

6. Do you think Kathy's parents are old-fashioned because they don't want her to marry Bob? Explain your answer.

    _____

    _____

7. How do you think Kathy's parents will react to her engagement?

    _____

    _____

8. What do you think they will say to her?

    _____

    _____

SYNONYMS

Synonyms are words that have the same or a similar meaning. In the blank spaces, write a synonym for the underlined word or words.

have to	**views**	**starving**	**attractive**	**around**
am crazy about	**get**	**darling**	**a lot of**	**too**

1. The children are very hungry. _____starving_____
2. We don't have much money. _____
3. Where can I obtain a map of the city? _____
4. It's late. We must leave soon. _____
5. The pants cost about $30. _____
6. I love my baby sister. _____
7. Nicole is very pretty. _____
8. Frank is coming to the dance, and his sister is coming also.
   _____
9. Steve and Chris have similar ideas about education. _____
10. Do you want anything, dear? _____

ANTONYMS

Antonyms are words that have opposite meanings. In the blank spaces, write an antonym for each word.

wonderful	**lose**	**foolish**	**stop**	**after**
late	**together**	**more**	**handsome**	**always**

1. start _____stop_____
2. separately _____
3. find _____
4. ugly _____
5. terrible _____
6. never _____
7. wise _____
8. early _____
9. less _____
10. before _____

2

FOOD
AND
WORK

It's Easy to Open a Can of Spaghetti

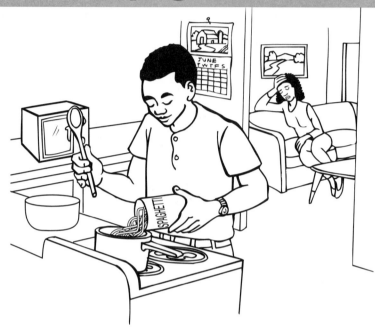

1. **calm** *v.* to quiet; to make peaceful   "The doctor gave Jonathan some medicine to <u>calm</u> his nerves."
2. **can** *n.* a metal container used to hold food   "We have a <u>can</u> of corn and a <u>can</u> of tomatoes."
3. **fever** *n.* a body temperature higher than normal (98.6° Fahrenheit)   "I feel hot. I think I have a <u>fever</u>."
4. **How about . . . ?** *idiom* an expression used to ask if a person would like something   "<u>How about</u> a piece of chocolate cake?"
5. **kid** *v.* to joke   "The President is coming to visit us!"   "You must be <u>kidding</u>." "Yes, I am. He's not coming."
6. **lie down** *v.* to put the body in a flat position   "Katie is tired. She's going to <u>lie down</u> for an hour."
7. **should** *v.* to be the correct thing to do; to be a good idea   "Nick has a toothache. He <u>should</u> go to the dentist."
8. **upset** *adj.* feeling sick because one's stomach is not right: be very unhappy   "Gina can't eat now. She has an <u>upset</u> stomach."   "My dog died. I'm very <u>upset</u>."

PREVIEW QUESTIONS

Discuss these questions before reading the dialog.

1. Can you cook? Do you like to cook?
2. How often do you cook?
3. Are you a good cook?

Tom and Rita are married. Tom comes home from work. Rita doesn't feel well. Tom wants her to rest, but she thinks she should cook supper for him. Tom offers to cook, but he's not a good cook. However, it's easy for him to open a can of spaghetti.

Rita: Hi, Tom. How was your day?

Tom: Fine. And yours?

Rita: I had a bad day.

Tom: What's the problem?

Rita: I have a fever and a headache.

Tom: That's too bad. [1]

Rita: And my stomach is upset.

Tom: You should call the doctor.

Rita: I'll call after supper.

Tom: Why don't you lie down and rest?

Rita: I can't lie down now.

Tom: Why not?

Rita: I have to cook your supper.

Tom: I'll cook supper.

Rita: Are you kidding? You can't cook.

Tom: No, but I can open a can of spaghetti. That's easy.

Rita: Good idea, but I can't eat spaghetti tonight.

Tom: I know. What can I get you?

Rita: Some toast, please.

Tom: And how about a cup of tea?

Rita: Good. That will calm my stomach.

---

1. The expression **too bad** often indicates that we feel sorry about something.   "It's <u>too bad</u> that Alex is sick."

COMPREHENSION

Answer these questions in pairs or small groups. Use your own ideas to answer questions with an asterisk.

1. How does Tom feel? And Rita?
2. What's wrong with Rita?
3. What is she going to do after supper?
4. What does she say she has to do?
*5. Today more men know how to cook than in the past. Why?
*6. Why can't Rita eat spaghetti tonight?
7. What is she going to have for supper?

DIALOG REVIEW

Complete the paragraphs with these words.

idea	too bad	kidding	fever	can
should	has to	calm	lie down	upset

Rita had a bad day. She has a _____ and a headache, and her stomach is _____. Tom says that's _____ and thinks she _____ call the doctor. He also wants her to _____ and rest.

Rita says she _____ cook Tom's supper. He offers to cook. She thinks that's impossible, but he isn't _____. He can open a _____ of spaghetti.

Rita thinks that's a good _____, but she can't eat spaghetti tonight. So Tom is going to make her some toast and tea to _____ her stomach.

SHARING INFORMATION

Discuss these questions in pairs or small groups.

1. How do you feel today?
2. Rita has a headache. How often do you get headaches? Frequently? Sometimes? Rarely? Never?
3. When you get a headache, do you take any medicine? What do you take? Does it help much?
4. When your stomach is upset, do you eat anything? If so, what?
5. What do you drink when your stomach is upset?
6. What time do you usually eat supper?
7. In some countries, people eat their main meal in the afternoon and a smaller meal in the evening. What time do people usually eat their main meal in your country?
8. Why do people spend less time cooking today than in the past?
9. Do you like spaghetti? Do you eat it often? Is it easy to cook?
10. Do you like to kid people? Do you do it often?

DICTATION

1. *Listen while the teacher reads the dialog without stopping.* <u>*Don't write anything*</u>.

2. *The teacher will read the dialog a second time, pausing after the missing lines.* <u>*Write in the missing lines*</u>.

3. *The teacher will read the dialog a third time.* <u>*Check your work*</u>.

Tom: What's the problem?

Rita: _____

Tom: That's too bad.

Rita: _____

Tom: You should call the doctor.

Rita: _____

Tom: Why don't you lie down and rest?

Rita: _____

Tom: Why not?

Rita: _____

The Chicken Smells Good

WORD PREVIEW

1. **be back** *idiom* to return "Kimberly is leaving, but she'll <u>be back</u> in an hour."
2. **decaffeinated** (often shortened to **decaf**) *adj.* without caffeine, for example, *decaffeinated* coffee and *decaffeinated* tea "Caffeine keeps me awake at night. That's why I drink <u>decaffeinated</u> coffee."
3. **dessert** *n.* sweet food served at the end of a meal, for example, pie, cake "We're having apple pie for <u>dessert</u>."
4. **dressing** *n.* a sauce put on salads to make them taste better "This salad needs more <u>dressing</u>."
5. **else** *adv.* more; in addition "What <u>else</u> do you want?"
6. **few** *adj.* a small number of "Heather ate a <u>few</u> cookies."
7. **loaf (of bread)** *n.* bread baked in one piece "Colin went to the store to get a <u>loaf of bread</u>."
8. **patient** *adj.* able to wait calmly "The cafeteria lines are long, and they move slowly. We'll have to be <u>patient</u>."
9. **quart** *n.* a measure for liquids = 1/4 gallon "I'm going to buy a <u>quart</u> of orange juice."
10. **regular** *adj.* ordinary "Our <u>regular</u> teacher was absent today. We had a substitute."
11. **sound** *v.* to seem "Your job <u>sounds</u> interesting."

PREVIEW QUESTIONS

Discuss these questions before reading the dialog.

1. Do you like chicken and rice? Do you have it often?
2. Who cooks your dinner?
3. What's your favorite dessert?

Denise comes home from work. She's very hungry. Her husband, Rick, is cooking chicken and rice for dinner.   They need coffee, milk, and bread. Rick asks Denise to go to the store.   She goes and returns quickly.

Denise: What are we having for dinner?

Rick: Chicken, rice, and a salad.

Denise: That sounds good. What's for dessert?

Rick: Your favorite. Vanilla ice cream.

Denise: Great! I'm starving.

Rick: Can you go to the store for me?

Denise: Sure. What do you need?

Rick: A quart of milk and coffee.

Denise: Regular or decaf?

Rick: Decaf.

Denise: Anything else?

Rick: Yes, one more thing. A loaf of bread.

Denise: OK. See you later.

(15 minutes later)

Rick: You're back fast.

Denise: Of course. I'm hungry!

Rick: What do you want on your salad?

Denise: French dressing. When will dinner be ready?

Rick: In a few minutes, dear. Be patient.

Denise: Mmm—the chicken smells good!

TRUE OR FALSE

If the sentence is true, write T. *If it's false, write* F.

_____ 1. Denise's favorite dessert is cake.

_____ 2. She likes chicken and rice.

_____ 3. She's very hungry.

_____ 4. Rick asks her to get a lot of food at the store.

_____ 5. He doesn't care what kind of coffee she gets.

_____ 6. Denise returns from the store quickly.

_____ 7. She doesn't want anything on her salad.

_____ 8. Rick asks her to be patient.

DIALOG REVIEW

Complete the paragraphs with these words.

quart	patient	dessert	else	sounds
loaf	starving	few	smells	regular

Rick is cooking dinner. His wife, Denise, asks him what they're having. He tells her they're having chicken, rice, and a salad. That _____ good to her.   And for _____ , they're having vanilla ice cream. Denise can't wait to eat. She's _____ .

Rick asks Denise to go to the store to get a _____ of milk and some coffee. He doesn't want _____ coffee; he wants decaf. Denise asks him if he wants anything _____ . He asks her to get a _____ of bread.

Denise goes to the store and returns quickly. She's very hungry. Rick tells her to be _____ .   Dinner will be ready in a _____ minutes.   She says that the chicken _____ good.

SHARING INFORMATION

Discuss these questions in pairs or small groups.

1. Are you hungry?
2. Do you like salad? What do you usually put on your salad?
3. What is your favorite dinner?
4. Do you like ice cream? Do you eat it often?
5. What flavors do you like?
6. Do you drink coffee? Do you drink it often?
7. Do you drink regular coffee or decaf?
8. Does caffeine keep you awake at night?
9. Should husbands and wives take turns cooking? Explain your answer.
10. Do husbands often cook in your country? Explain your answer.

STORY COMPLETION

Fish and Apple Pie

Nancy and Scott are going out for dinner. The restaurant is near their house. They want to get home by 9:00.

Complete the story with these words.

few	dessert	decaf	favorite
smells	be back	starving	of course

...d Scott are going to their
...only a _____
_____ home by

...he's _____ .

...r dinner and apple pie for
_____ , apple pie has a lot of

_____ coffee.

...o good!

All Bosses Are Demanding

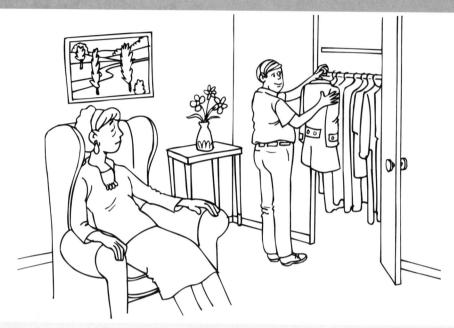

1. **angry** *adj.* feeling anger (*Anger* is a strong feeling one gets when offended or disturbed by another.) "Why are you <u>angry</u> at Sam? What did he do?"
2. **at least** *idiom* if nothing else "Roger isn't a good baseball player, but <u>at least</u> he tries."
3. **complain** *v.* to say that one is unhappy because something is not the way one wants it "A lot of students <u>complain</u> about the food in the cafeteria."
4. **demanding** *adj.* requiring a lot of work "Mr. Trawinski is a <u>demanding</u> teacher. We have to do a lot of work for his class."
5. **hard** *adv.* with much effort "Pamela studies very <u>hard</u>."
6. **like** *prep.* similar to "Roberta looks a lot <u>like</u> her sister."
7. **pay** *n.* the money one receives for the work one does "If we work extra hours, we get extra <u>pay</u>."
8. **slave** *n.* a person who is owned by another; a person completely controlled by another "You can't make me do all that work. I'm not your <u>slave</u>."
9. **so** *conj.* for that reason; since that is true "We were hungry, <u>so</u> we stopped to eat."
10. **take it easy** *idiom* relax "I work hard all week, but on Saturday I like to <u>take it easy</u>."
11. **treat** *v.* to act toward "The company <u>treats</u> its workers well."
12. **turn** *n.* the time when one should do something "It's my <u>turn</u> to wash the dishes."
13. **wrong** *adj.* not as something should be; not as one wanted "Sue is crying. I wonder what's <u>wrong</u>."

PREVIEW QUESTIONS

Discuss these questions before reading the dialog.

1. Is there a time of day when you usually feel tired? When?
2. How often do you get angry? Frequently? Sometimes? Not much? Almost never?
3. Who do you get angry at?

Irene is tired when she arrives home from work. She's also angry at her boss. She had a hard day. Her husband, Frank, is understanding, but he reminds her that she has a good job.

Frank:	Hi, Irene! How's everything?
Irene:	Not good. I'm tired and angry!
Frank:	What's wrong?
Irene:	Work, work, work! I work too hard!
Frank:	Let me take your jacket.
Irene:	Thanks, honey.
Frank:	Sit down and take it easy.
Irene:	I don't like my boss.
Frank:	Why not?
Irene:	She's too demanding.
Frank:	But all bosses are demanding.
Irene:	I know, but my boss treats me like a slave.
Frank:	What do you mean?
Irene:	She's always telling me to do this and do that.
Frank:	Well, at least you have a good job.
Irene:	True, and my pay is good.
Frank:	So what more do you want?
Irene:	Supper and a handsome husband!
Frank:	You have a handsome husband.
Irene:	And who's cooking tonight?
Frank:	It's my turn.
Irene:	Maybe I complain too much.
Frank:	I think so.[1]

1. **So** is frequently used in place of repeating previous words. Here, *so* takes the place of *you complain too much.* "I think so." = "I think *you complain too much.*"

COMPREHENSION

Answer these questions in pairs or small groups. Use your own ideas to answer questions with an asterisk.

1. Why is Irene tired and angry?
2. Why doesn't she like her boss?
3. How does she feel that her boss treats her?
*4. Do you think Irene's boss is just doing her job, or is she too demanding? Explain your answer.
5. Irene has a good job and gets a good salary. What more does she want?
6. Who's cooking tonight?
*7. Do you think Irene complains too much? Explain your answer.

DIALOG REVIEW

Complete the paragraphs with these words.

take it easy	**slave**	**turn**	**demanding**	**so**
at least	**angry**	**treats**	**complain**	**hard**

Irene is tired and _____ when she arrives home from work. She thinks she works too _____ . Her husband takes her jacket and tells her to sit down and _____ .

Irene doesn't like her boss. She says she's too _____ and that she _____ her like a _____ . Frank tells her that _____ she has a good job.

Irene wants to know who's cooking dinner. Frank tells her that it's his _____ . Irene says she may _____ too much. Frank thinks _____ .

SHARING INFORMATION

Discuss these questions in pairs or small groups.

1. Complete this sentence. I get angry when _____.
2. Circle the words that describe what a good boss should be. Explain your answers. (a) good-looking (b) smart (c) good at making decisions (d) rich (e) understanding
3. Do you think your boss (your teacher) is demanding?
4. What often happens if a boss isn't demanding?
5. Is it important that a teacher be demanding? Explain your answer.
6. What do you do when you're tired and want to relax?
7. Do you think Frank is a good husband? Explain your answer.
8. What do people usually complain about?
9. What do you complain about?
10. How often do you complain? Frequently? Sometimes? Rarely? Never?

MATCHING

Match the words in Column A with their definitions or descriptions in Column B. Print the letters on the blank lines.

Column A

_____ 1. fever
_____ 2. dressing
_____ 3. patient
_____ 4. demanding
_____ 5. kid
_____ 6. quart
_____ 7. else
_____ 8. pay
_____ 9. should
_____ 10. slave
_____ 11. can
_____ 12. dessert

Column B

A. more
B. a person owned by another
C. to joke
D. pie, cake, ice cream
E. a high temperature
F. money we receive for work
G. able to wait calmly
H. it holds food
I. there are four in a gallon
J. what we put on salad
K. to be a good idea
L. requiring a lot of work

Ice Cream, Candy, and Potato Chips

1. **appetite** *n.* a desire to eat "My son is always hungry. He has a good <u>appetite</u>."
2. **cooperate** *v.* to work together "It's nice to work in an office where everyone <u>cooperates</u>."
3. **gain** *v.* to get more of something; to increase "The best way to <u>gain</u> customers is to lower prices."
4. **own** *v.* to have; to possess "Rebecca is rich. She <u>owns</u> two houses, three cars, and a boat."
5. **pleasant** *adj.* nice "We had a <u>pleasant</u> trip."
6. **quite** *adv.* very (but not as strong as *very*); somewhat "Jason is <u>quite</u> tall."
7. **rarely** *adv.* not often "I <u>rarely</u> watch TV in the morning."
8. **still** *adv.* up to and at this time (*Still* indicates that an action or situation continues.) "Mario is <u>still</u> working." "Barbara is <u>still</u> in the hospital."

PREVIEW QUESTIONS

Discuss these questions before reading the story.

1. What country and city are you from?
2. How long ago did you come to the United States?
3. How do you feel about your weight?
   (a) It's OK. (b) I want to gain weight. (c) I want to lose weight.

Gloria is 34 years old and was born in Havana, Cuba. She came to the United States when she was 14 and married Pete eight years later. Gloria and Pete are very happy and have two children, Carlos and Sandra. Carlos is ten and Sandra is eight.

Gloria owns a dress shop in Miami, Florida. She's an excellent businesswoman, and her shop is very busy. She works hard and makes a lot of money.

Everyone likes Gloria. She's a very warm person. She's always friendly and has a pleasant smile. She cooperates with everyone and rarely gets angry. But she has one big problem.

She can't control her appetite. She loves foods that have a lot of calories, and she especially likes ice cream, candy, and potato chips. Gloria gained 15 pounds last year and now weighs 180, but she's still quite attractive. She doesn't want to be thin, but she would like to lose 30 pounds.

Gloria is going on a diet today—her third this year. When she starts a diet, she eats lots of vegetables, chicken, and fish. She doesn't have any ice cream, candy, or potato chips. In a few weeks, however, she gets tired of her diet and starts to eat everything again. "It's going to be different this time," she says. "I'm going to get more exercise, eat less, and lose 30 pounds." It won't be easy, but she's going to try.

TRUE OR FALSE

If the sentence is true, write T. *If it's false, write* F.

_____ 1. Gloria came to the United States from Cuba when she was 14.

_____ 2. She owns a restaurant in Miami, Florida.

_____ 3. Her business is doing well.

_____ 4. She's friendly and has a nice smile.

_____ 5. She gets angry a lot.

_____ 6. She weighs 180 pounds, but is still pretty.

_____ 7. She wants to be thin.

_____ 8. She can easily lose 30 pounds.

STORY COMPLETION

Tony and Sal

Tony and Sal have an Italian restaurant in Chicago, and it's very popular. Although they're good friends, Tony and Sal are also very different. Tony is thin and doesn't eat much. Sal weighs 200 pounds and loves to eat.

Complete the story with these words.

exercise	lots of	appetite	still
quite	rarely	own	gains

Tony and Sal _____ an Italian restaurant in Chicago. They opened the restaurant ten years ago, and it _____ makes _____ money.

Although Tony and Sal are good friends, they're also _____ different.

Tony is very thin and never _____ weight. He's careful about what he eats and gets a lot of _____ .

Sal has a big _____ , weighs 200 pounds, and _____ gets any exercise.

SHARING INFORMATION

Discuss these questions in pairs or small groups. Space is provided to write your answers if you wish.

1. How far is it from Havana, Cuba to Miami, Florida?

    _____

    _____

2. Why have a large number of Cubans come to the United States?

    _____

    _____

3. Do you think that most people who own their own business work long hours? Explain your answer.

    _____

    _____

4. Do people who have their own business often make a lot of money? Do some lose a lot?

    _____

    _____

5. Plain potatoes don't have a lot of calories, but potato chips do. Why? Do you like potato chips?

    _____

    _____

6. Vegetables are good for everyone. Do you like them? What are your favorites?

    _____

    _____

7. Do you like fish? What kind of fish do you eat? Do you eat fish often?

    _____

    _____

8. Do you think Gloria will stay on her diet this time? Explain your answer.

    _____

    _____

Pete Loves Sports and Gambling

1. **benefit** *n.* anything a person receives for work in addition to money "My job has good <u>benefits</u>—a long vacation, 15 sick days a year, and health insurance."
2. **bet** *v.* to put money on a game or numbers, for example, lottery numbers "I <u>bet</u> ten dollars on a baseball team. I hope the team wins."
3. **count on** *idiom* to trust; to rely on "You can <u>count on</u> me to help you clean up after the party."
4. **fan** *n.* a person with a special interest in a sport or team "Lisa is a tennis <u>fan</u>."
5. **gamble** *v.* to take a chance, especially by putting money on a game or numbers "Many people go to casinos to <u>gamble</u>."
6. **get along (with)** *idiom* to be friendly (with) "I <u>get along with</u> Craig."
7. **gymnastics** *n.* a sport in which athletes show their strength and balance by doing special exercises "<u>Gymnastics</u> is a very popular sport in the Olympics."
8. **insurance** *n.* an agreement that a person will be paid money in case of sickness, accident, or death "Rashid has $50,000 worth of life <u>insurance</u>."
9. **jog** *v.* to run for exercise "Leslie likes to <u>jog</u> after work."
10. **lottery** *n.* a type of gambling, often run by the government, in which a person buys a ticket with numbers "If I win the <u>lottery</u>, I'll be rich."
11. **miss** *v.* to be absent "Amanda <u>missed</u> school yesterday. She was sick."
12. **pension** *n.* the money a person receives when he or she stops working "When I'm 65, I'll get a good <u>pension</u>."
13. **pretty** *adv.* quite "The accident was <u>pretty</u> bad."
14. **racetrack** *n.* a place where horses race "Andy loves to go to the <u>racetrack</u>."
15. **reliable** *adj.* a person or thing one can trust "Toyotas are very <u>reliable</u> cars."
16. **twice** *adv.* two times "I brush my teeth <u>twice</u> a day."
17. **weakness** *n.* a strong desire for something "Tim has a <u>weakness</u> for ice cream."

PREVIEW QUESTIONS

Discuss these questions before reading the story.

1. What's your favorite sport?
2. Do you play any sports? Which ones?
3. Some people bet a lot of money on sports. What's the problem with this?

Pete is 36 years old and works for the post office. He has worked there for 12 years. His salary is good, and his benefits are excellent. All postal workers have health insurance and a good pension plan.

Pete works hard, rarely misses work, and is never late. He's reliable, and his supervisors know that they can count on him. He also gets along well with the other workers.

Pete loves sports. He played football and baseball in high school, and he still jogs three or four times a week. Football is his favorite sport, and in the fall, he watches a lot of football on TV. Sometimes he takes the family to see the Miami Dolphins[1] play. They're big Dolphins fans.

Pete's son, Carlos, also loves football and baseball, but baseball is his favorite sport. He plays baseball all summer in a park near his house, and he's pretty good. He wants to play football too, but he's still too young. Sandra, Pete's daughter, likes gymnastics and takes lessons twice a week. She also plays softball and is one of the better players on the team.

Pete doesn't drink or smoke, but he has one big weakness. He loves to gamble. He buys a lottery ticket every day. He goes to the racetrack every week. He also bets on football, basketball, and baseball games. Sometimes he wins a lot of money, but sometimes he loses a lot. This makes his wife, Gloria, angry. "You should stop betting," she tells Pete. "I'll stop betting if you lose 40 pounds," he replies.

1. The **Miami Dolphins** are a professional football team. They play in the National Football League.

COMPREHENSION

Answer these questions in pairs or small groups. Use your own ideas to answer questions with an asterisk.

1. Where does Pete work? How long has he worked there?
2. Name two benefits he receives.
3. How often does he miss work? How often is he late?
4. What exercise does he still do?
5. What two sports does Carlos like? And Sandra?
6. What is Pete's one big weakness?
*7. Do you think he should stop betting? Explain your answer.
*8. Do you think he will? Explain your answer.

STORY COMPLETION

Darryl Loves Basketball

Darryl loves basketball and plays on the high-school team. He's always at practice and tries very hard. He's a big help to the team and the coach.

count on	fan	twice	misses
better	gets along with	reliable	pretty

Darryl is a basketball _____ and also plays on the high-school team. He's _____ good, but some of the other players on the team are _____. _____ this year, he scored 20 points in a game.

Darryl is friendly and _____ everyone on the team.

He never _____ practice or a game and tries very hard.   The team and the coach can always _____ him. He's very _____.

SHARING INFORMATION

Discuss these questions in pairs or small groups. Space is provided to write your answers if you wish.

1. Do you jog? If so, how often? Does it make you feel better?

   _____

   _____

2. What sports are popular in your country? Which is the most popular?

   _____

   _____

3. Name three countries, not including the United States, in which baseball is very popular.

   _____

   _____

4. Do you watch sports on TV? Which ones?

   _____

   _____

5. Do schools give girls as many opportunities to play sports as they do boys? If not, why don't they?

   _____

   _____

6. Did you ever go to a horse race? If so, was it fun?

   _____

   _____

7. What is a lottery? Do you buy lottery tickets? How often?

   _____

   _____

8. If you won a million dollars in a lottery, what would you do with the money?

   _____

   _____

SYNONYMS

Synonyms are words that have the same or a similar meaning. In the blank spaces, write a synonym for the underlined word or words.

cooperate	ready	jog	be back	of course
pleasant	a job	maybe	can	gamble

1. <u>Perhaps</u> we should wait for Denise. _____
2. "Are you going to the dance?" "<u>Certainly</u>. I love to dance."
   _____
3. We had a <u>nice</u> walk. _____
4. Sun-Hi <u>is able to</u> speak Korean and English. _____
5. Are the children <u>prepared</u> to leave for school? _____
6. Al likes to <u>bet</u>, but I don't. _____
7. Michelle is looking for <u>work</u>. _____
8. Dustin will <u>return</u> this afternoon. _____
9. We have to learn to <u>work together</u>. _____
10. Kristin and Ashley <u>run</u> a mile every day. _____

ANTONYMS

Antonyms are words that have opposite meanings. In the blank spaces, write an antonym for each word.

easy	win	weakness	true	fast
love	few	rare	take	everything

1. false _____
2. many _____
3. nothing _____
4. difficult _____
5. strength _____
6. hate _____
7. give _____
8. lose _____
9. slow _____
10. frequent _____

3

ACHES AND PAINS

Heart Trouble Is Always Serious

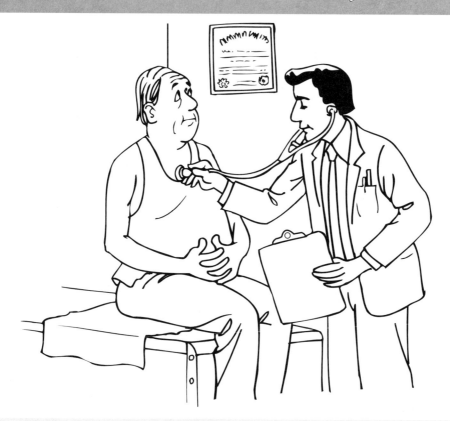

1. **beer** *n.* an alcoholic drink made from grain   "Stan had a <u>beer</u> at the party."
2. **guess** *v.* to think something is probable; to believe   "Our history teacher is absent. I <u>guess</u> she's sick."
3. **have got to** *idiom* have to; must   "We <u>have got to</u> clean the basement—it's very dirty."
4. **pain** *n.* a feeling of discomfort in part of the body   "I can't throw the ball. I have a <u>pain</u> in my shoulder."
5. **relax** *v.* to rest; to not worry   "After dinner, Hiroko likes to <u>relax</u> and watch TV."
6. **right away** *idiom* immediately   "Danielle called the police <u>right away</u>."
7. **right now** *idiom* immediately (*Right* gives emphasis to *now*. *Right away* and *right now* are similar in meaning.)   "If you don't leave <u>right now</u>, you're going to be late for work."
8. **trouble** *n.* a problem; an illness   "I'm having <u>trouble</u> with my back. I have got to see a doctor."
9. **What's the matter?** *idiom* What's the problem?; What's wrong?   "<u>What's the matter</u> with the elevator?"

PREVIEW QUESTIONS

Discuss these questions before reading the dialog.

1. What would you do if you had a pain in your chest, and it didn't go away?
2. Do you worry much about your health? Explain your answer.
3. Smoking is bad for your lungs. Do you know that it's also bad for your heart?

    Kevin has pains in his chest, so he goes to the doctor. The doctor discovers that Kevin has heart trouble. He tells Kevin he must stop smoking and lose weight. His wife, Linda, gets upset when she hears about Kevin's heart trouble.

Linda:	How do you feel, Kevin?
Kevin:	I still have the pains in my chest.
Linda:	When are you going to the doctor?
Kevin:	Right now.
Linda:	Do you want me to drive you?
Kevin:	No, I can drive. You stay home and take care of the baby.

          (Two hours later, Kevin returns home.)

Linda:	What did the doctor say?
Kevin:	I'll be fine, but I must stop smoking.
Linda:	Why? What's the matter?
Kevin:	A little heart trouble. It's nothing serious.
Linda:	Heart trouble is always serious.
Kevin:	You worry too much. I'll be OK.
Linda:	So when are you going to stop smoking?
Kevin:	Right away!
Linda:	Great! What else did the doctor say?
Kevin:	I have to lose 25 pounds.
Linda:	No cake or cookies for you, dear!
Kevin:	Then get me a beer, please.
Linda:	But doesn't beer have a lot of calories?
Kevin:	I guess it does, but I've got to[1] relax!

---

1. **I've got to** is a contraction for *I have got to.*

COMPREHENSION

Answer these questions in pairs or small groups. Use your own ideas to answer questions with an asterisk.

1. Why is Kevin going to the doctor?
2. What does the doctor tell him to stop?
3. What's wrong with Kevin?
4. When is he going to stop smoking?
5. What else does the doctor want him to do?
*6. Do you think heart trouble is always serious? Explain your answer.
*7. Linda is worried about Kevin. Do you think Kevin is also worried? Explain your answer.

DIALOG REVIEW

Complete the paragraphs with these words.

matter	right away	lose	still	worries
relax	pains	trouble	else	must

Linda asks Kevin how he feels. He tells her he _____ has the _____ in his chest.

Kevin goes to a doctor, and the doctor tells him that he _____ stop smoking. When he tells Linda this, she wants to know what's the _____. He tells her it's a little heart _____ and is nothing serious. But she says that heart trouble is always serious. Kevin thinks she _____ too much.

Linda wants to know when Kevin is going to stop smoking. He says he's going to stop _____. She also wants to know what _____ the doctor said. Kevin tells her that the doctor wants him to _____ 25 pounds.

Linda tells Kevin there will be no more cake or cookies for him. He asks for a beer. He knows beer has a lot of calories, but he says he's got to _____.

SHARING INFORMATION

Discuss these questions in pairs or small groups.

1. Many people go to a doctor once a year for a general examination. Why is that a good idea?
2. How much do doctors usually charge for a visit to their office?
3. Sometimes pain helps us. How?
4. Name some things that people worry about.
5. Do you think that everyone worries? Explain your answer.
6. Complete this sentence. Sometimes I worry about _____ .
7. Why is it important to have someone we can talk to about our worries?
8. Do you smoke? If so, when did you start, and why?
9. Why is it difficult to stop smoking?
10. Why is extra weight bad for our heart?

DICTATION

1. *Listen while the teacher reads the dialog without stopping.* <u>*Don't write anything*</u>.

2. *The teacher will read the dialog a second time, pausing after the missing lines.* <u>*Write in the missing lines*</u>.

3. *The teacher will read the dialog a third time.* <u>*Check your work*</u>.

Linda: What did the doctor say?

Kevin: _____

Linda: Why? What's the matter?

Kevin: _____

Linda: Heart trouble is always serious.

Kevin: _____

Linda: So when are you going to stop smoking?

Kevin: _____

Linda: Great! What else did the doctor say?

Kevin: _____

Put on Plenty of BENGAY

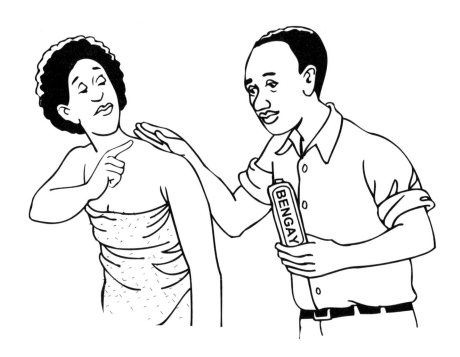

1. **BENGAY**® *n.* a medicine one puts on sore muscles to lessen the pain "My arm is sore from playing baseball. I'm going to put some BENGAY on it."
2. **deny** *v.* to say that something is not true "The teacher thinks that Jeff copied from Ronny during the exam, but Jeff denies it."
3. **enough** *adj.* as much as needed "We don't have enough money to buy that house."
4. **kill** *v.* to hurt very much "I walked a lot today, and my feet are killing me."
5. **plenty (of)** *adj.* a lot (of) "Mrs. Lee is rich. She has plenty of money."
6. **rub** *v.* to move one's hand back and forth over something "The nurse is rubbing Erica's back with alcohol."
7. **spoil** *v.* to do too much for a person "Everyone in the family spoils the baby."
8. **spot** *n.* a place "This is a nice spot for a picnic."
9. **way** *n.* manner "I don't like the way you're acting."

PREVIEW QUESTIONS

Discuss these questions before reading the dialog.

1. What is BENGAY?
2. Do you ever use BENGAY or a similar product?
3. Husbands and wives often help one another with their little problems. Do you think this is important to a happy marriage? Explain your answer.

Paula has a bad pain in her shoulder. She tells her husband, Reggie, about the pain. He gets some BENGAY from the bathroom cabinet and rubs it on her shoulder. Reggie tells Paula that he's spoiling her. She says that's OK. She spoils him sometimes.

Paula:	I have a pain in my shoulder.
Reggie:	Is the pain bad?
Paula:	Very—my shoulder is killing me!
Reggie:	Is there anything I can do?
Paula:	Do we have any BENGAY?
Reggie:	Yes, in the bathroom cabinet.
Paula:	Would[1] you rub some on my shoulder?
Reggie:	Sure. I'll get it right now.
Paula:	Thanks, dear. That will really help.
Reggie:	Are you ready for the BENGAY?
Paula:	Yes, put on plenty. The pain is terrible!
Reggie:	OK. Is this the right spot?
Paula:	A little closer to my neck, please.
Reggie:	All right. How does that feel?
Paula:	Great! Put on a little more.
Reggie:	Is that enough?
Paula:	That's fine.
Reggie:	I shouldn't spoil you this way.
Paula:	Why not? I spoil you sometimes.
Reggie:	I can't deny that.

---

1. **Would** is often used to introduce a polite request. "Would you close the door, please?" "Would you mail this letter for me?"

COMPREHENSION

Answer these questions in pairs or small groups. Use your own ideas to answer questions with an asterisk.

1. How bad is the pain in Paula's shoulder?
2. Where is the BENGAY?
3. How much BENGAY does Paula want?
4. How does the BENGAY feel?
*5. Paula could have put the BENGAY on herself. Why didn't she?
*6. Paula says she also spoils Reggie. What does she mean?
7. What can't Reggie deny?

DIALOG REVIEW

Complete the paragraphs with these words.

closer	**killing**	**spot**	**deny**	**rub**
plenty	**way**	**shoulder**	**terrible**	**shouldn't**

Paula has a pain in her _____ . She asks her husband, Reggie, to _____ some BENGAY on it. Her shoulder is _____ her.

Reggie gets the BENGAY from the bathroom cabinet. Paula asks him to put on _____ . She says the pain is _____ . He asks if he is putting the BENGAY in the right _____ . She asks him to put it a little _____ to her neck.

Reggie tells his wife he _____ spoil her in this _____ . She wants to know why not. She spoils him sometimes. He can't _____ that.

SHARING INFORMATION

Discuss these questions in pairs or small groups.

1. Do you ever get sore muscles or pains like Paula?
2. What usually causes sore muscles?
3. If you get a headache, do you take any medicine? If so, what?
4. Does the medicine help much?
5. Do you think that, at times, a husband should spoil his wife, and she should spoil him? Explain your answer.
6. Reggie is helpful when Paula wants a little care and attention. Are most husbands helpful in such situations?
7. Do parents often spoil their children?
8. How do they spoil them?
9. Why do they spoil them?
10. Is it bad to spoil children? If so, why?

STORY COMPLETION

A Very Bad Day

When Derek got up this morning, he had a headache, and on the way to work, he got into an accident. He was going 75 miles an hour.

Complete the story with these words.

shoulder	**deny**	**way**	**killing**
spot	**terrible**	**enough**	**shouldn't**

When Derek got up this morning, he had a _____ headache. The pain was _____ him, so he took two aspirin. And that was just the beginning of a very bad day.

On the way to work, Derek had an accident and hurt his _____. He tried to stop before he hit the car in front of him, but he didn't have _____ time.

The police say Derek was going 75 miles an hour, and he doesn't _____ it. He knows he _____ go so fast. Last week he almost had an accident in the same _____ on the highway. Derek has to change the _____ he drives.

A Pain in the Side

WORD PREVIEW

1. **appendicitis** *n.* a condition in which the appendix is inflamed (red and sore) "I have a pain in my right side. I hope it's not <u>appendicitis</u>."
2. **appendix** *n.* part of the large intestine, extending three or four inches from the intestine on the right side of the body "The doctor had to remove Gary's <u>appendix</u>."
3. **at once** *idiom* immediately "I called the fire department, and they came <u>at once</u>."
4. **awful** *adj.* very bad "The movie was <u>awful</u>. No one liked it."
5. **emergency** *n.* a situation that develops suddenly and needs immediate attention "We need your help! Come quickly! It's an <u>emergency</u>!"
6. **hardly** *adv.* almost not; only a little "I can't tell you much about Sally. I <u>hardly</u> know her."
7. **how** *adv.* to what degree (*How* followed by an adjective often introduces a question.) "<u>How</u> tall are you?" "<u>How</u> long is the movie?"
8. **patient** *n.* a person receiving care from a doctor "The doctor is examining a <u>patient</u>."

PREVIEW QUESTIONS

Discuss these questions before reading the dialog.

1. The appendix is part of our body. Where is it?
2. Did you ever have to have your appendix removed?
3. Can appendicitis be dangerous?

Steve has a pain in his side and a fever. He calls Dr.[1] Marina Lesko. The nurse answers the phone. Steve tells the nurse about his pain and fever. The nurse talks to Dr. Lesko, and the doctor sends Steve to the hospital. He may have appendicitis.

Nurse: Good afternoon. Dr. Lesko's office.

Steve: Hi, this is Steve Campos. I'm a patient of Dr. Lesko.

Nurse: Yes, Mr. Campos. I remember. This is Dr. Lesko's nurse.
         How can I help you?

Steve: I have a fever and a pain in my right side.

Nurse: Tell me exactly where the pain is.

Steve: It's near my appendix.

Nurse: Is the pain very bad?

Steve: It's awful. I can hardly walk.

Nurse: How high is your temperature?

Steve: One hundred and two.[2]

Nurse: All right. Let me talk to the doctor.

Steve: Thank you.

                    (a few minutes later)

Nurse: Is your wife home, Mr. Campos?

Steve: Yes, she is.

Nurse: Good. Can she drive you to the hospital?

Steve: Yes. To what hospital?

Nurse: To the emergency room of The General Hospital.

Steve: Why? What's wrong? What did the doctor say?

Nurse: You may have appendicitis.

Steve: Oh, no!

Nurse: Yes, go to the hospital at once.

---

[1]. **Dr.** is an abbreviation for doctor. "Dr. Marina Lesko" = "Doctor Marina Lesko"
[2]. In the United States, we usually measure temperature with a Fahrenheit thermometer. The letter F indicates Fahrenheit. **One hundred and two** in this line means 102 degrees Fahrenheit (102° F); 98.6° is the normal temperature of the body on the Fahrenheit scale.

COMPREHENSION

Answer these questions in pairs or small groups. Use your own ideas to answer questions with an asterisk.

1. Why is Steve Campos calling Dr. Lesko's office?
2. Where exactly is his pain?
3. Is it very bad?
4. What is Steve's temperature?
5. Where does Dr. Lesko send him?
*6. How will Steve's wife feel when he tells her that he may have appendicitis?
*7. What will she probably say to him?

DIALOG REVIEW

Complete the paragraphs with these words.

emergency	**exactly**	**hardly**	**may**	**side**
awful	**at once**	**patient**	**near**	**temperature**

Steve Campos is a _____ of Dr. Marina Lesko.   He calls her office and speaks with the nurse.

He tells the nurse he has a fever and a pain in his right _____.   She wants to know _____ where the pain is.   He tells her it's _____ his appendix. She asks how bad the pain is.   He tells her it's _____ and that he can _____ walk. He also has a _____ of 102° F.

The nurse talks to Dr. Lesko.   The doctor sends Steve to the _____ room of The General Hospital.   She thinks he _____ have appendicitis.   She wants him to go _____ .

SHARING INFORMATION

Discuss these questions in pairs or small groups.

1. Does medical science know why the body has an appendix?
2. Is it important to go to the same doctor so that he or she gets to know you?
3. Do you think your doctor is good? Do you like him or her?
4. Is it important to you to have a doctor that speaks your first language?
5. Were you ever a patient in a hospital in your country? If so, for how long?
6. In your opinion, how good is the care in most hospitals in your country?
7. Hospital rooms in the United States are expensive. Are they also expensive in your country?
8. Who pays the hospital bills in your country? The government? Insurance? The patient?
9. Were you ever a patient in a hospital in the United States? If so, for how long?
10. In your opinion, how good is the care in most hospitals in the United States?

MATCHING

Match the words in Column A with their definitions or descriptions in Column B. Print the letters on the blank lines.

Column A

_____ 1. deny

_____ 2. way

_____ 3. awful

_____ 4. relax

_____ 5. hardly

_____ 6. beer

_____ 7. spoil

_____ 8. patient

_____ 9. at once

_____ 10. appendix

_____ 11. kill

_____ 12. plenty

Column B

A. to rest

B. a lot

C. to do too much for someone

D. part of the body

E. manner

F. to hurt a lot

G. immediately

H. very bad

I. an alcoholic drink

J. to say something isn't true

K. a person who goes to a doctor

L. only a little

A Busy Manager

1. **ambitious** *adj.* having a strong desire for success, money, and power   "Carmen wants to get a better job and to make a lot of money. She's ambitious."
2. **breathing** *n.* the movement of air in and out of the lungs   "Something is wrong with the baby's breathing. I'm taking him to the hospital."
3. **crowded** *adj.* many people in one place   "The trains are crowded at five p.m."
4. **handle** *v.* to work with; to deal with   "Let me talk to Ben. I know how to handle him."
5. **hectic** *adj.* very busy   "The first day of class is always hectic."
6. **major** *adj.* very important   "Route 80 is a major highway."
7. **manager** *n.* a person who directs others; a supervisor   "If you can't help me, I would like to speak to the manager, please."
8. **overweight** *adj.* having too much weight   "Don weighs 250 pounds. He's 70 pounds overweight."
9. **pace** *n.* rate of speed   "Robin likes to work at a slow pace."
10. **pack** *n.* a small package of items, for example, a pack of gum, matches, or cigarettes   "I have two packs of gum. Take one."
11. **rapid** *adj.* fast   "The company is growing at a rapid rate."
12. **severe** *adj.* serious   "Mary Lou has a severe headache."
13. **slice** *n.* a thin piece cut from a larger piece, for example, a slice of bread   "Please put a slice of cheese on my hamburger."
14. **workaholic** *n.* a person addicted to work   "Alexei works 12 hours a day, six days a week! He's a workaholic."
15. **worse** *adj.* comparative of the adjective *bad*   "My toothache is getting worse. I'm going to call the dentist."

PREVIEW QUESTIONS

Discuss these questions before reading the story.

1. Do you think that the manager of a large department store has a demanding job? Explain your answer.
2. An alcoholic is a person who can't control the desire to drink, who is addicted to alcohol. What is a <u>work</u>aholic? What is a <u>choc</u>oholic?
3. Do you think a workaholic is happier working or lying on the beach? Explain your answer.

Ed is the manager of a large department store. He's 42. He works hard and is ambitious. He wants his store to be the best. It's a busy store, and it's always crowded. Ed's job is demanding, and the pace is hectic. He has to handle all of the store's major problems.

Ed doesn't take care of his health. He smokes two packs of cigarettes a day, is 40 pounds overweight, never gets any exercise, and is a heavy drinker. He also likes to stay up late and watch TV, and sometimes he doesn't get enough sleep.

When Ed got up yesterday, he didn't feel well. His wife, Alice, wanted him to stay home, but Ed doesn't like to miss work. He's a workaholic, and he thinks the store can't run without him.

Ed had his usual breakfast—a cup of black coffee, two slices of toast, and a cigarette. He kissed his wife good-bye and told her not to worry. He was at work by 8:30.

During the morning, Ed felt worse. He had severe pains in his chest and arms. His stomach was upset, and his breathing was rapid. He spoke to Hank, the assistant manager, and Hank took him home immediately.

TRUE OR FALSE

If the sentence is true, write T. *If it's false, write* F.

_____   1. Ed's store isn't doing well.

_____   2. He has a difficult job.

_____   3. He smokes and drinks a lot.

_____   4. He likes to go to bed early.

_____   5. He often goes for a walk or run in the park.

_____   6. He weighs too much.

_____   7. Alice wanted him to go to work.

_____   8. While at work, he had a problem with his breathing.

STORY COMPLETION

The Vice Principal

Mr. Romano is the vice principal of a large high school. He's always busy, and the students like him. He works 11 hours a day and is never absent. He hopes to be principal of the high school some day.

Complete the story with these words.

workaholic	**crowded**	**ambitious**	**misses**
worse	**hectic**	**health**	**handling**

Mr. Romano is the vice principal of Lincoln High School. He's always busy, and this week was especially _____ .

Mr. Romano is very good at _____ teenagers, and the students like him.   He's also _____ and wants to be the principal of the high school some day.

He gets to school at seven a.m. and stays to six p.m.   He's a _____ and never _____ work. Fortunately, he has very good _____ .

Lincoln High School was built for 1200 students, but now it has more than 2,000, and many of the classes are _____ . Next year, there will be even more students, and the situation will be _____ .

SHARING INFORMATION

Discuss these questions in pairs or small groups. Space is provided to write your answers if you wish.

1. Ed had an upset stomach and pains in his arms as well as in his chest. Are these problems common when a person has a heart attack?

    _____

    _____

2. Do you think Ed should have called the doctor from work? Explain your answer.

    _____

    _____

3. Which would you prefer: a job as a manager with long hours, a lot of responsibility, and very good pay, or a job as an assistant manager with shorter hours, less responsibility, and less pay? Explain your answer.

    _____

    _____

4. What advice would you give to a workaholic like Ed?

    _____

    _____

5. Do you think that workaholics often neglect their families? Explain your answer.

    _____

    _____

6. Do you like to stay up late to watch TV or to read? If so, what do you like to watch or read?

    _____

    _____

7. How much sleep do you usually get?

    _____

    _____

8. How much sleep do you think you should get?

    _____

    _____

A Hug and a Kiss

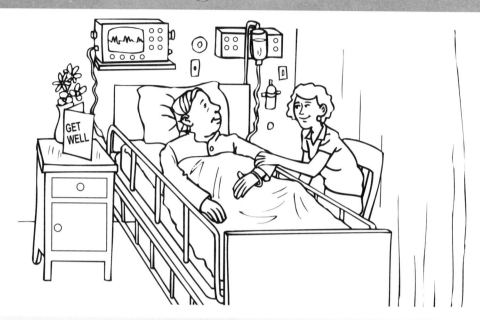

1. **allow** *v.* to say that it's OK to do something; to permit "They won't <u>allow</u> you to smoke on the plane."

2. **calm** *adj.* quiet and peaceful "After the accident, I tried to stay <u>calm</u>, but it was impossible."

3. **cardiologist** *n.* a doctor who specializes in heart problems "Ever since Tony had a heart attack last year, he has been going to a <u>cardiologist</u>."

4. **condition** *n.* the state of one's health "The doctor examined me and said I was in excellent <u>condition</u>."

5. **coronary** *adj.* having to do with the heart or the arteries that carry blood to the heart "Regular exercise and a low-fat diet will help keep your <u>coronary</u> arteries healthy."

6. **fortunately** *adv.* by good luck; luckily "<u>Fortunately</u>, we had nice weather for the picnic."

7. **gentle** *adj.* soft; not rough or violent "Mr. Klein is <u>gentle</u> with his kids."

8. **heart attack** *n.* a condition in which the blood going to the heart is blocked "Call 911—I have pains in my chest! I think I'm having a <u>heart attack</u>."

9. **hug** *n.* the action of putting one's arms around another "Tiffany gives her children a <u>hug</u> and kiss before they leave for school."

10. **oxygen** *n.* a gas that is present in air and water "Gene can't breathe. He needs <u>oxygen</u>."

11. **treat** *v.* to give medical help to "The doctor <u>treated</u> me for the flu."

12. **unit** *n.* an independent group that is also part of a larger group; a division "Abdul is in the intensive care <u>unit</u> of Columbus Hospital. He was in a terrible auto accident."

PREVIEW QUESTIONS

Discuss these questions before reading the story.

1. Why is it so important to get to a doctor immediately if you're having a heart attack?
2. Most hospitals have a coronary care unit. What is a coronary care unit?
3. What special services does it have?

As soon as Ed arrived home, his wife called the doctor. She described Ed's condition. The doctor listened carefully and said that Ed should go to the hospital at once. Alice tried to stay calm, but she was very nervous. She drove Ed to the emergency room of the hospital.

Ed's doctor was there waiting for him. He examined Ed and told Alice that Ed had a heart attack. They took him to the coronary care unit and gave him oxygen. A cardiologist came and treated Ed.

Alice sat in the emergency waiting room for two hours and worried. Then the doctors allowed her to visit her husband for ten minutes. She was so happy to see him again. She gave him a gentle hug and a kiss. He smiled and held her hand. Fortunately, Ed's heart attack wasn't too bad.

Ed should be able to leave the hospital after a week of rest and care. However, there will be many changes in his life. He will have to stop smoking, get more rest, and lose weight. There will be no more heavy drinking or late-night TV.

Ed asked the doctor when he could go back to work. "You should be able to go back in six weeks," the doctor replied. "But you must learn to work less and relax more." That won't be easy!

COMPREHENSION

Answer these questions in pairs or small groups. Use your own ideas to answer questions with an asterisk.

*1.   Why didn't Ed call the doctor?
 2.   What did the doctor say to Alice?
 3.   What did the doctor tell her in the hospital?
 4.   How long did the doctors allow her to visit Ed?
 5.   What did she give him?
 6.   What changes will Ed have to make?
 7.   When should he be able to go back to work?
*8.   Why will it be difficult for him to work less and relax more?

STORY COMPLETION

A Good Nurse

Valerie is a nurse in a hospital in New York City. She's very good to the patients and doesn't get upset easily, but she's tired at the end of the day. When she gets home, she reads the newspaper and relaxes.

condition	treat	fortunately	unit
arrives	as soon as	hug	calm

Valerie is a nurse at St. Luke's Hospital in New York City. She works in the intensive care _____. _____ she starts work, she checks the _____ of her patients.

_____, Valerie is a very _____ person who doesn't get upset easily and who knows how to _____ patients.

By the end of the day, Valerie is very tired. She leaves the hospital at 4:30 and _____ home around five. She gives her husband a _____, reads the newspaper, and relaxes.

SHARING INFORMATION

Discuss these questions in pairs or small groups. Space is provided to write your answers if you wish.

1. Do you think Ed should get a job that is less demanding? Do you think he will? Explain your answers.

   _____

   _____

2. What kind of exercise do you think would be good for Ed? Explain your answer.

   _____

   _____

3. People who don't smoke are usually very sensitive to smoke. Does it bother you if someone near you smokes?

   _____

   _____

4. Do you know anyone who stopped smoking? Did the person feel better? Did the person start smoking again?

   _____

   _____

5. Although a glass of wine can be good for the heart, heavy drinking is not. What other part of the body is often hurt by heavy drinking?

   _____

   _____

6. A cardiologist is a heart specialist. Today many doctors are specialists. Why is this good?

   _____

   _____

7. Having many kinds of specialists is good, but what problem can this cause?

   _____

   _____

8. Specialists make a lot of money. Some people think they make too much. Others say they deserve what they make. What do you think?

   _____

   _____

SYNONYMS

Synonyms are words that have the same or a similar meaning. In the blank spaces, write a synonym for the underlined word or words.

all right	allow	little	near	right away
else	spot	rapid	enough	great

1. Ricky is only a <u>small</u> boy. _____
2. That was a <u>very good</u> play. _____
3. Is it <u>OK</u> if I use your phone? _____
4. Let's sit <u>close to</u> the window. _____
5. This is a good <u>place</u> to fish. _____
6. Four dozen cookies will be <u>sufficient</u> for the party. _____
7. They don't <u>permit</u> alcohol in the park. _____
8. I want to talk to you <u>immediately</u>. _____
9. What <u>more</u> do you want? _____
10. Chen is a <u>fast</u> worker. _____

ANTONYMS

Antonyms are words that have opposite meanings. In the blank spaces, write an antonym for each word.

deny	large	high	major	leave
full	remember	hectic	heavy	pain

1. minor _____
2. forget _____
3. pleasure _____
4. low _____
5. admit _____
6. light _____
7. small _____
8. enter _____
9. empty _____
10. peaceful _____

4

FAMILIES AND PETS

A Brown Puppy

Animal Shelter

WORD PREVIEW

1. **animal shelter** *n.* a place that cares for lost animals and animals no one owns. "There are many cats and dogs at the <u>animal shelter</u>."
2. **belong** *v.* to be in the right place "That chair <u>belongs</u> in the kitchen."
3. **charge** *v.* to ask as a price "The taxi driver <u>charged</u> $20 to take me to the airport."
4. **come on** *idiom* let's start moving "<u>Come on</u>. We have to go home."
5. **feed** *v.* to give food to "Charley is <u>feeding</u> the baby."
6. **kind** *n.* type "What <u>kind</u> of fish do you like?"
7. **loyal** *adj.* to be faithful or true to one's family, friends, or country "Mohammed has many <u>loyal</u> friends. They'll help him."
8. **mall** *n.* an enclosed shopping center with many stores "Kathy and I like to shop at the <u>mall</u>."
9. **pet** *n.* an animal that lives in a home as a companion "Dogs are very popular <u>pets</u>."
10. **puppy** *n.* a very young dog "<u>Puppies</u> love to play."
11. **terrier** *n.* a small, active dog, originally used in hunting "Our <u>terrier</u> likes to run in the yard."
12. **train** *v.* to teach a person or animal by practice "They're <u>training</u> the employees to use the new computer system."

PREVIEW QUESTIONS

Discuss these questions before reading the dialog.

1. If you don't have a dog, would you like one? What kind of dog would you like?
2. Where can a person get a dog?
3. Do you think it's better to get a dog from a pet shop or an animal shelter? Explain your answer.

Young Soo is 12, and he wants to get a dog. His mother doesn't like the idea, but Young Soo promises to take good care of the dog. His mother finally says OK, and they get a cute brown puppy from an animal shelter.

Young Soo:	Mom, can we get a dog?
Mother:	I don't think so.
Young Soo:	Why not? They're so friendly and loyal.
Mother:	Who's going to train it, feed it, and walk it?
Young Soo:	I will.
Mother:	That's what you say now, but . . .
Young Soo:	Honest,[1] Mom, I'll take good care of it.
Mother:	What kind of dog do you want?
Young Soo:	A big one.
Mother:	Absolutely not! Big dogs belong in the country.
Young Soo:	OK, we can get a small dog, like a terrier.
Mother:	Where are we going to get it?
Young Soo:	From the pet shop at the mall.
Mother:	We should call the animal shelter first.
Young Soo:	Good idea! They won't charge much.

(later at the animal shelter)

Mother:	Look at that little brown puppy. It's so cute!
Young Soo:	Can we get it? Please!
Mother:	OK, but don't forget your promise.
Young Soo:	Don't worry, I won't. What shall[2] we call her?
Mother:	How about Sandy?
Young Soo:	Perfect. Come on, Sandy. Let's go!

1. **Honest** is usually an adjective and means *not lying* or *stealing*, but here, *honest* is an adverb and means *really* or *believe me*. This is an informal use of *honest*. "Honest, Dad, I'll be home early."
2. In the future tense, we often use **shall** when we ask questions that have *I* or *we* as the subject. "What shall I say to him?" "What shall we do?"

COMPREHENSION

Answer these questions in pairs or small groups. Use your own ideas to answer questions with an asterisk.

1. What does Young Soo want?
2. What does his mother want to know before they get a dog?
3. What kind of dog does Young Soo want?
*4. Why does his mother say that big dogs belong in the country?
5. How much will it cost to get a dog from the animal shelter?
*6. Do you think Young Soo's mother likes dogs? Explain your answer.
7. What do they name the dog? *Why are *brown* dogs often named Sandy?

DIALOG REVIEW

Complete the paragraphs with these words.

animal shelter	like	loyal	charge	train
kind	puppy	mall	belong	pet

Young Soo asks his mother if they can get a dog. He tells her dogs are very friendly and _____, but his mother wants to know who's going to _____ it, feed it, and walk it. He says he will.

Young Soo's mother asks him what _____ of dog he wants. He wants a big one, but his mother tells him absolutely not. She says that big dogs _____ in the country.

Young Soo asks if they can get a small dog, _____ a terrier. His mother wants to know where they're going to get it. He tells her from the _____ shop at the _____, but his mother says they should call the _____ first. Young Soo thinks that's a good idea because they won't _____ much.

Young Soo and his mother look at a little, brown _____. It's cute, and Young Soo wants to get it. His mother says OK, but she tells him not to forget his promise to take good care of the dog.

SHARING INFORMATION

Discuss these questions in pairs or small groups.

1. Does a dog need much care? Explain your answer.
2. Many children want dogs. Do you think it's good for a child to have a dog? Explain your answer.
3. About how much do you think it costs to buy a dog from a pet shop?
4. Many apartments don't allow people to have dogs. Why not?
5. Do dogs see better than people? Do they hear better? Do they have a better sense of smell?
6. About how long does a dog live?
7. Many police departments have dogs. What do these dogs do?
8. Are most dogs good at protecting their owners and their homes? How do they protect them?
9. Why do we say that a dog is man's best friend?
10. What other animals are often pets?

DICTATION

1. *Listen while the teacher reads the dialog without stopping. <u>Don't write anything</u>.*

2. *The teacher will read the dialog a second time, pausing after the missing lines. <u>Write in the missing lines</u>.*

3. *The teacher will read the dialog a third time. <u>Check your work</u>.*

Mother:	Where are we going to get a dog?
Young Soo:	_____
Mother:	We should call the animal shelter first.
Young Soo:	_____

(later at the animal shelter)

Mother:	Look at that little, brown puppy. It's so cute!
Young Soo:	_____
Mother:	OK, but don't forget your promise.
Young Soo:	_____
Mother:	How about Sandy?
Young Soo:	_____

A Famous Cherry Tree

1. **ax** *n.* a tool with a long handle and metal head used to cut down trees "The farmer is cutting down the tree with an <u>ax</u>."
2. **cherry** *n.* a small, round fruit that is sweet and usually red "Have some <u>cherries</u>. They taste great."
3. **chop down** *v.* to keep hitting a tree with an ax until the tree falls "The tree is dying. We should <u>chop</u> it <u>down</u>."
4. **fun** *n.* what gives a person pleasure "It's <u>fun</u> to dance."
5. **gee whiz** *idiom* a very informal expression used especially by children to show surprise, or that they're unhappy about something "<u>Gee whiz</u>, Dad, do I have to go to bed so early?"
6. **how** *adv.* that is very (*How* followed by an adjective is often used to give special emphasis to the adjective.) "<u>How</u> nice!" = "That's very nice!" "<u>How</u> interesting!" = "That's very interesting!"
7. **kid** *n.* a child "I'm taking the <u>kids</u> to the park."
8. **lie** *n.* a statement one makes knowing it isn't true "Ruth says that she cleaned her room, but that's a <u>lie</u>. It's still dirty."
9. **lie** *v.* to make a statement that one knows isn't true "Leo is 60, and sometimes he <u>lies</u> about his age."
10. **plant** *v.* to put seeds, plants, or very young trees in the ground "We're going to <u>plant</u> corn in our vegetable garden."
11. **stupid** *adj.* not intelligent; foolish "It's <u>stupid</u> to drive after drinking alcohol."
12. **truth** *n.* the facts; what is true "Tell me the <u>truth</u>. Did you break the window?"
13. **yard** *n.* the ground around a house "The children are playing in the <u>yard</u>."

PREVIEW QUESTIONS

Discuss these questions before reading the dialog.

1. Complete this sentence. George Washington was the first _____ of the United States.
2. Name some places and things named after Washington.
3. They say that George Washington never lied. Maybe that's true, but people often lie. Why do people lie?

There is a famous story that George Washington chopped down a cherry tree when he was a boy. When his parents asked if he chopped down the tree, he told them he did it. He said he couldn't lie to them. Our dialog tells the same story, but in a different way.

Mother:	George, come here!
George:	I'm coming, Mother.
Mother:	I can't find the ax. Did you see it?
George:	Yes, it's in my room.
Mother:	What's it doing there?
George:	I used it to chop down a tree.
Mother:	What tree?
George:	The cherry tree in our back yard.
Mother:	Don't tell me you chopped down our cherry tree!
George:	Yes, I did.
Mother:	Why?
George:	For fun.
Mother:	How stupid! Your father is going to be angry at you.
George:	No, he won't.
Mother:	He certainly will! He planted that tree when he was a boy.
George:	But I'll tell him some other kid did it.
Mother:	That's a lie![1] George, you can't lie to your father.
George:	Gee whiz, Mother! Do I always have to tell the truth?
Mother:	Of course, you do! Washingtons[2] never lie.

---

1. In this line, **lie** is used as a noun, "That's a lie!" and as a verb, "George, you can't lie to your father."
2. **Washingtons** = the members of the Washington family. *Washingtons* is the plural of *Washington*.

TRUE OR FALSE

If the sentence is true, write T. *If it's false, write* F.

_____ 1. Mrs. Washington is looking for the ax George used.

_____ 2. The ax is in the basement.

_____ 3. Mrs. Washington is happy that George chopped down the cherry tree.

_____ 4. He chopped it down because he needed some wood.

_____ 5. The cherry tree was behind the house.

_____ 6. Mrs. Washington planted the cherry tree many years ago.

_____ 7. George was going to lie to his father.

_____ 8. Mrs. Washington tells George he must always tell the truth.

DIALOG REVIEW

Complete the paragraphs with these words.

cherry	angry	truth	yard	find
lie	fun	chop down	planted	stupid

Mrs. Washington can't _____ the ax. Her son George says it's in his room because he used it to _____ a tree. His mother asks him what tree. He tells her it was the _____ tree in their back _____ .

His mother asks him why he did this. George says he did it for _____ . She says that was _____ , and that his father is going to be _____ at him because his father _____ that tree when he was a boy.

George says he's going to tell his father that some other kid did it, but his mother tells him he can't _____ to his father. He has to tell the _____ . Washingtons never lie.

SHARING INFORMATION

Discuss these questions in pairs or small groups.

1. A legend is a story from the past, often about a great hero. Do you think that the legend about Washington and the cherry tree is true? Explain your answer.
2. All countries have famous heroes. Name the most famous hero or heroes of your country.
3. What did that hero or those heroes do?
4. In our dialog, why was George Washington going to lie to his father?
5. Do people who lie to keep out of trouble often get into worse trouble? Explain your answer.
6. Name two things that are fun to do.
7. A person who gets angry quickly is sometimes called a "hot head." Do you know any hot heads? Are you one?
8. How often do you get angry? (a) frequently (b) sometimes (c) rarely (d) almost never
9. Name one thing that others do that makes you angry.
10. Name something that makes teachers angry.

STORY COMPLETION

A Beautiful Garden

Mr. Rana has a big garden, and he loves to work in it. The garden has many beautiful flowers, and he often tells the children not to play in it.

Complete the story with these words.

planting	angry	cherry	how
chop down	yard	finds	fun

Mr. Rana has a garden in his _____, and he likes to work there. He says it's _____. Today he is _____ flowers in the garden.

There is also an old _____ tree in the yard, but he plans to _____ the tree so that the flowers will get more sun.

Mr. Rana often warns the children not to play in his garden, and he gets _____ if he _____ them there.

Many people tell Mr. Rana _____ beautiful his garden is.

Kids Are Different Today

1. **couple (of)** *n.* a small number; a few   "It's a <u>couple of</u> miles to the next gas station."
2. **heartbroken** *adj.* very sad; filled with great sorrow   "Marty's girlfriend doesn't want to see him anymore. He's <u>heartbroken</u>."
3. **joke** *n.* something a person says or does to make others laugh   "Roy's <u>jokes</u> always make me laugh."
4. **normal** *adj.* natural; usual   "Brenda doesn't like to get up early. That's <u>normal</u>."
5. **slap** *n.* the act of hitting with an open hand   "Lillian gave her daughter a <u>slap</u> on the hand."
6. **slap in the face** *idiom*   an insult   "Doris didn't invite her cousin to her wedding. It was a <u>slap in the face</u>."

PREVIEW QUESTIONS

Discuss these questions before reading the dialog.

1. Some women leave home before they marry. Why?
2. What often makes it difficult or impossible for them to leave?
3. Do you think that most young women in the United States leave home before marriage? Or do most stay home?

Amy is a dental assistant. She's 21 years old. Edna, her mother, is very strict. Amy decides to leave home and to rent an apartment with her friend Beth. Amy's mother is very upset. She's discussing the situation with her brother, Mike.

Edna: Hi, Mike. How are you?

Mike: Great! And you?

Edna: I'm very upset!

Mike: What's the matter?

Edna: Amy's leaving home.

Mike: Is she getting married?

Edna: No! She's just moving out of the house.

Mike: You must be kidding!

Edna: It's no joke.

Mike: Where's she going to live?

Edna: She's renting an apartment with her friend Beth.

Mike: I'm sorry to hear this.

Edna: Amy's so young. I'm heartbroken. It's a slap in the face.

Mike: I understand.

Edna: I never thought she would[1] do this to me.

Mike: Don't worry. She'll be back in a couple of months.

Edna: I hope so.[2]

Mike: Why's she leaving?

Edna: She says she wants to be her own boss.

Mike: That's normal. Most girls feel that way by the time they're 21.

Edna: Sure, but they don't leave home.

Mike: Some do. Kids are different today.

---

1. In this sentence, **would** is the past of *will*. The past is used because *would do* depends on a verb *(thought)* that is past. "I *know* Joe *will* come." "I *knew* Joe *would* come."
2. In this line, **so** is used in place of repeating the previous line, "She'll be back in a couple of months."

COMPREHENSION

Answer these questions in pairs or small groups. Use your own ideas to answer questions with an asterisk.

1. Why is Edna upset?
2. Is Amy getting married?
3. Where is she going to live?
*4. What bills will Amy and Beth have to pay that they probably didn't pay before?
5. When does Mike think Amy will be back?
*6. Do you think she'll come back? Explain your answer.
7. Why's she leaving?

DIALOG REVIEW

Complete the paragraphs with these words.

be back	renting	couple	slap	joke
heartbroken	own	just	so	thought

Edna is very upset. Her daughter, Amy, is leaving home, but she's not getting married. She's _____ moving out of the house. When Edna tells her brother, Mike, about Amy, he thinks she's kidding, but it's no _____ .

Amy is _____ an apartment with her friend Beth. Edna says she's _____ , and that Amy's leaving is a _____ in the face. She never _____ Amy would do this to her.

Mike thinks Amy will _____ in a _____ of months. Edna hopes _____ .

Amy says she's leaving home because she wants to be her _____ boss.

SHARING INFORMATION

Discuss these questions in pairs or small groups.

1. Do many young women in your country leave home before marriage?
2. Do you think it's OK for a young person to leave home before marriage? Explain your answer.
3. It will be expensive for Amy and Beth to live away from home. What are some other problems they may have?
4. What are some advantages in leaving home before marriage?
5. Do you feel sorry for Edna? Why or why not?
6. Do you think that most parents get very upset when a daughter or son leaves home before marriage? Explain your answer.
7. When a son or daughter leaves home before marriage, are there advantages for the parents? If so, what advantages?
8. Some parents are too protective of their children. They don't give them enough freedom. Give an example of this.
9. Some parents give their children too much freedom. Give an example.
10. Do you think children are different today? If so, how?

MATCHING

Match the words in Column A with their definitions or descriptions in Column B. Print the letters on the blank lines.

Column A		Column B	
_____ 1.	kind	A.	to ask as a price
_____ 2.	cherry	B.	to teach by practice
_____ 3.	normal	C.	to tell someone what you know is untrue
_____ 4.	couple (of)	D.	what farmers do in the spring
_____ 5.	charge	E.	a very young dog
_____ 6.	pet	F.	a few
_____ 7.	lie (verb)	G.	type
_____ 8.	joke	H.	the facts
_____ 9.	puppy	I.	usual
_____ 10.	train	J.	a good one makes people laugh
_____ 11.	truth	K.	a small, round fruit
_____ 12.	plant (verb)	L.	an animal that's a companion

Three Children, a Dog, and a Cat

1. **admit** *v.* to say you did something wrong or made a mistake "Randy <u>admitted</u> that he took the money."
2. **annoy** *v.* to make another person angry; to disturb "It <u>annoys</u> me when people phone to sell me things I don't want."
3. **bark** *v.* to make the sound a dog makes "Our dog always <u>barks</u> at the letter carrier."
4. **bite** *v.* to put one's teeth into "Don't <u>bite</u> your fingernails."
5. **boring** *adj.* not interesting; dull "No one liked the show. It was <u>boring</u>."
6. **business administration** *n.* the study of the ways of running a business "My brother teaches <u>business administration</u> at Boston College."
7. **captain** *n.* the leader of a team "Shirley is the <u>captain</u> of the volleyball team."
8. **fresh** *adj.* not showing respect "Phil gets very angry when his son is <u>fresh</u>."
9. **grade** *n.* the level of a class in school "Rachel is in the seventh <u>grade</u>."
10. **senior** *n.* a person in the last year of high school or college "My daughter is a <u>senior</u> in college. She'll graduate this year."
11. **soccer** *n.* a game in which you advance the ball by kicking it (It's called *football* in most countries, but *soccer* in the United States.) "We hope our team wins the <u>soccer</u> game."
12. **stranger** *n.* a person one does not know at all "I never saw that man before. He's a <u>stranger</u>."
13. **subject** *n.* an area of study, for example, science, history, geography, English "History is my favorite <u>subject</u>."
14. **tail** *n.* the part of an animal's body that extends from its rear "Rabbits have large ears and small <u>tails</u>."
15. **wag** *v.* to move back and forth (used especially to describe a dog moving its tail) "When my dog <u>wags</u> her tail, I know she's happy."

PREVIEW QUESTIONS

Discuss these questions before reading the story.

1. Do you have a dog or cat? Why do so many people have dogs or cats as pets?
2. Do you like math? Are you good at it?
3. What is (was) your favorite subject or subjects in school?

Carol and Mark are married and have two boys and a girl. The girl's name is Erin, and the boys' names are Tim and Alex. They also have a dog named Lucky and a cat named Tabby.

Erin is 17, and she's the oldest child. She's a senior in high school and will graduate in June.   She's an excellent student and the captain of the basketball team. "I plan to go to college and to study computer science or business administration," she says. "I also want to play basketball in college and hope I can make the team."

Tim is 12 and is in the seventh grade.   He does well in school, but he thinks it's boring. Math is the only subject he enjoys.   He also likes to play soccer, but music is his first love.   He plays the piano and the guitar very well.   He's shy and quiet.

Alex is eight and is the baby of the family.   Everyone spoils him, especially Carol.   He's in the third grade and thinks school is fun, but he frequently gets in trouble in school.   Carol won't admit it, but he can be fresh, and the teachers don't like that.

Lucky is a friendly dog and wags his tail a lot.   He barks at strangers, but he never bites. Lucky is 12, which is old for a dog, and he's getting fat. Tabby is a young and active cat who is always playing and jumping. Sometimes she annoys Lucky, but they're good friends.

TRUE OR FALSE

If the sentence is true, write T. *If it's false, write* F.

_____ 1. Carol and Mark have three children, two dogs, and a cat.

_____ 2. Erin does very well in school.

_____ 3. Tim thinks that school is interesting.

_____ 4. He doesn't talk much.

_____ 5. Carol is strict with Alex.

_____ 6. Alex enjoys school, but he gets in trouble a lot.

_____ 7. Although he barks, there is no reason to be afraid of Lucky.

_____ 8. Tabby is a lazy cat.

STORY COMPLETION

A Dog Named Max

Jerry and Nicole have a three-year-old daughter named Sarah and a dog named Max. Max is a big, friendly dog, but many people are afraid of him. Sarah likes to play with Max.

Complete the story with these words.

strangers	**annoys**	**shy**	**tail**
enjoys	**spoil**	**bite**	**barks**

Jerry and Nicole have a three-year-old daughter named Sarah and a dog named Max. Jerry and Nicole love Sarah and Max, and they _____ them.

Max is a big dog and _____ a lot, but he's friendly. However, _____ don't know that, and most of them are afraid of him.

Sarah is _____ and doesn't have a lot of friends, but she _____ playing with Max, and sometimes she pulls his _____ . This _____ Max, and Nicole tells her to stop.

Nicole knows Max would never _____ Sarah, but it's important to teach her to treat Max the right way.

SHARING INFORMATION

Discuss these questions in pairs or small groups. Space is provided to write your answers if you wish.

1. Erin plans to study computer science or business administration in college. Do you think there are many jobs available in the field of computers?

    _____

    _____

2. Are many jobs available in the field of business administration? teaching? nursing?

    _____

    _____

3. What job would you like to have? Why?

    _____

    _____

4. Do you think school is fun or boring? or both? Explain your answer.

    _____

    _____

5. Do you plan to go to college? If so, what do you want to study?

    _____

    _____

6. Tim loves music. Do you like to listen to music? What kind of music do you like?

    _____

    _____

7. What kind of music is popular in your country?

    _____

    _____

8. Can you play a musical instrument? If so, which one(s)?

    _____

    _____

Mark and Carol

1. **article** *n.* a story in a newspaper or magazine "In yesterday's paper, there was a very interesting article about computers."
2. **bookkeeper** *n.* a person who keeps financial records for a business "The bookkeeper keeps a record of the money our company receives and spends."
3. **dangerous** *adj.* anything that can easily hurt someone "Football is a dangerous sport; tennis is not."
4. **drive crazy** *idiom* to disturb very much "That loud music is driving me crazy!"
5. **fit** *v.* to be the right size "This jacket fits perfectly."
6. **hate** *v.* to dislike a lot "Shawn hates to clean his room."
7. **historic** *adj.* a place or thing that is important in history "There are many historic buildings in Boston."
8. **junk** *n.* things that have no value "Why are you saving that old bicycle? It's junk."
9. **just** *adv.* exactly "What time is it?" "It's just three o'clock."
10. **nag** *v.* to correct often "Mrs. Wilson is always nagging her husband."
11. **neat** *adj.* keeping everything in order "Eva's closet is always neat."
12. **noon** *n.* twelve o'clock during the day "I have lunch from noon to one o'clock."
13. **opposite** *n.* a person or thing that is completely different from another "Matthew loves to talk; his brother is exactly the opposite. He's very quiet."
14. **pack rat** *n.* a type of rat that collects and keeps many small things in its nest: a person who collects and keeps many things that he or she doesn't need or use "Carl is a pack rat. He keeps old newspapers, letters, boxes, and clothes."
15. **passenger** *n.* a person (except the driver) riding in a bus, car, train, etc. "There were 15 passengers on the bus."
16. **route** *n.* the road(s) one takes to get from one place to another "What route do you take to get to work?"
17. **rush** *v.* to move fast; to hurry "Lew is rushing to get to the bank before it closes."
18. **slippery** *adj.* likely to cause one to fall, or a driver to lose control "The sidewalks and roads are icy and very slippery."
19. **sort** *n.* type; kind "Toys R Us sells all sorts of toys and games."
20. **throw out** *v.* to put in the garbage "I'm going to throw out these old shoes."

PREVIEW QUESTIONS

Discuss these questions before reading the story.

1. Do you think that bus drivers have a difficult job? Explain your answer.
2. Do you think that they have a good job? Explain your answer.
3. Do you spend much time talking on the phone? If so, who do you talk to?

Mark is a bus driver. He gets up at six o'clock, eats a light breakfast, and rushes to work. He has to be at the bus garage by 6.45. Mark lives and works in Philadelphia, and his bus route goes past Independence Hall[1] and other historic buildings.

Mark likes his work and is friendly with his passengers. His salary is good, and he also gets a lot of overtime. However, he hates to drive in the rain and snow. They make the roads slippery and dangerous.

Carol works every day from 8:30 to noon as a bookkeeper. In the afternoon, she shops, cleans the house, and picks up the children from school. She also likes to talk on the phone. She calls her sister almost every day, and they talk for an hour or more. Carol also calls her friends, and they call her. They talk about their children, their neighbors, and themselves.

Carol is very neat. She has a place for everything and throws out what she doesn't need. Mark is just the opposite; he saves everything. He's like a pack rat. He keeps clothes that don't fit anymore, old magazines, newspaper articles, boxes, and all sorts of junk. Nothing he has is in order. This drives Carol crazy. "I complain and nag Mark all the time," she says. "But he doesn't pay any attention. I don't think he'll ever change."

---

[1] **Independence Hall** is the building in Philadelphia where the Declaration of Independence was approved on July 4, 1776. "When you go to Philadelphia, make sure you visit <u>Independence Hall</u>."

COMPREHENSION

Answer these questions in pairs or small groups. Use your own ideas to answer questions with an asterisk.

1. Where does Mark live and work?
2. What does his bus route go past?
3. Why does he hate to drive in the rain and snow?
*4. Do you think that a bus driver's job is interesting or boring? Explain your answer.
5. What does Carol do in the morning? in the afternoon?
6. What do Carol and her friends talk about?
7. Name four things that Mark saves.
*8. Do you think that he will ever change? Explain your answer.

STORY COMPLETION

Complete the story with these words.

The President of the Bank

Mrs. Chung is the president of the Second National Bank. She goes to many meetings and does not like to be late for anything. Her secretary opens her mail and helps keep her desk in order.

hates	throws out	rushing	complain
nags	sorts	neat	junk

Mrs. Chung is the president of the Second National Bank. She has to attend many meetings, and she's always _____ to get to them on time. She _____ to be late for anything.

Mrs. Chung gets all _____ of mail. Some of it is very important, but much of it is _____. Her secretary opens the mail and _____ what's unimportant. This helps keep Mrs. Chung's desk and office _____.

If Mrs. Chung feels that bank employees aren't working hard enough, she _____ them to get them to work harder. Of course, they don't like this and they _____.

SHARING INFORMATION

Discuss these questions in pairs or small groups. Space is provided to write your answers if you wish.

1. What time do you usually get up in the morning? Do you have to rush to get to work or school on time?

   _____

   _____

2. Do you think that you talk more than, less than, or about the same amount as most people?

   _____

   _____

3. In general, who do you think talks more, men or women? If you think men talk more, why do they? If you think women talk more, why do they?

   _____

   _____

4. Do you usually save things, or do you usually throw things out? Are you more like Mark (the "pack rat") or more like Carol?

   _____

   _____

5. Are you good at keeping things neat, or are you more like Mark?

   _____

   _____

6. Why is it important to be neat?

   _____

   _____

7. Does anyone nag you? Who? Why?

   _____

   _____

8. Do you nag anyone? Who? Why?

   _____

   _____

SYNONYMS

Synonyms are words that have the same or a similar meaning. In the blank spaces, write a synonym for the underlined word or words.

belong	feed	shy	heartbroken	mall
neat	so	enjoy	frequently	kids

1. The <u>children</u> are watching TV. _____
2. Gina and Nick <u>like</u> swimming and tennis. _____
3. You're tired. You <u>should be</u> in bed. _____
4. Peggy's husband is in jail. She's <u>very sad</u>. _____
5. Don't <u>give food to</u> the animals. _____
6. They're opening a new store in the <u>shopping center</u>. _____
7. Sid's room is <u>in order</u>. _____
8. Cathy <u>often</u> gets headaches. _____
9. Pete makes new friends easily. He isn't <u>timid</u>. _____
10. It's <u>very</u> nice of you to visit us. _____

ANTONYMS

Antonyms are words that have opposite meanings. In the blank spaces, write an antonym for each word.

stupid	throw out	first	annoy	tail
famous	different	sorry	active	boring

1. same _____
2. head _____
3. smart _____
4. glad _____
5. unknown _____
6. please _____
7. interesting _____
8. last _____
9. passive _____
10. keep _____

5

ENGLISH AND JOBS

English Is a Crazy Language

WORD PREVIEW

1. **at least** *idiom*　maybe more, but not less; a minimum　"Jesse is <u>at least</u> 30 years old."
2. **catch** *v.* a.) to stop something with your hands and hold it　"Throw me the keys. I'll <u>catch</u> them." b.) to capture　"The police are trying to <u>catch</u> the thief." c.) to become sick with　"In the winter, many people <u>catch</u> the flu." d.) to be on time for　"Bill is leaving to <u>catch</u> his train."
3. **crazy** *adj.* very foolish　"You're <u>crazy</u> to go to work today. You're sick and should be in bed."
4. **pronounce** *v.* to say; to make the sound of a letter or word　"How do you <u>pronounce</u> this word?"
5. **pronunciation** *n.* the way in which a letter or word is said　"Akram's <u>pronunciation</u> of English is very good."
6. **several** *adj.* more than two, but not many　"We have visited Washington, D.C., <u>several</u> times."
7. **wonder** *n.* something very unusual; a surprise　"Bonnie is very smart and studies a lot. It's no <u>wonder</u> she got a 100 on the test."

PREVIEW QUESTIONS

Discuss these questions before reading the dialog.

1. Do you think that English is a difficult language to learn? Explain your answer.
2. Is it always difficult to learn a second language? Explain your answer.
3. Use the word *catch* in as many sentences as you can. (Webster's dictionary lists 18 meanings for the verb *catch*.)

Ivan and Akiko are studying English. They meet after class. Ivan tells Akiko that English is a crazy language. She smiles and asks Ivan to explain why he says that.

Ivan:	Hi, my name is Ivan, and I'm from Russia.
Akiko:	Nice to meet you, Ivan. My name is Akiko. I'm from Japan.
Ivan:	English is a difficult language, isn't it?[1]
Akiko:	A second language is always difficult.
Ivan:	True, but English is harder than most. It's a crazy language.
Akiko:	A crazy language?[2] Why do you say that?
Ivan:	One letter can have several pronunciations.
Akiko:	Can you give me an example?
Ivan:	Sure. Listen to the *o* in *hot, cold, love,* and *to.*
Akiko:	Hmm. They all sound different.
Ivan:	You see. There are at least four ways to pronounce *o.*
Akiko:	No wonder English is so hard.
Ivan:	And there's another problem with English.
Akiko:	What's that?
Ivan:	One word can have several meanings.
Akiko:	For example?
Ivan:	The verb *catch.* You say *to catch a ball* and *to catch a cold.*
Akiko:	They're very different.
Ivan:	And there's *to catch a bus* and *to catch a mouse.*
Akiko:	You're right, Ivan. English *is* a crazy language!

---

1. The addition of **isn't it** makes this sentence a question. Ivan expects Akiko to agree.
2. **A crazy language?** is a question. In informal English, we can make a word, or a group of words, a question by raising our voice at the end of the word or words.

COMPREHENSION

Answer these questions in pairs or small groups. Use your own ideas to answer questions with an asterisk.

1. What country is Ivan from? And Akiko?
2. What does Akiko say about a second language?
3. Why does Ivan say English is a crazy language?
4. Name four English words with different pronunciations of *o*.
*5. Do you think it's difficult to learn to pronounce English correctly? Explain your answer.
6. Ivan has another problem with English. What is it?
*7. Do you think English is a crazy language? Explain your answer.

DIALOG REVIEW

Complete the paragraphs with these words.

sound	meanings	crazy	wonder	example
several	pronounce	catch	at least	second

Ivan and Akiko are studying English. They meet after class. They agree that a _____ language is always difficult. Ivan says that English is a _____ language. Akiko asks him why he says that.

Ivan explains that one letter can have _____ pronunciations. Akiko wants him to give her an _____. He asks her to listen to the *o* in *hot, cold, love,* and *to.* They all _____ different.

Ivan tells Akiko that there are _____ four ways to _____ *o.* She says it's no _____ English is so hard.

Ivan tells Akiko that there is another problem with English. One word can have several _____. He gives her examples of four different ways to use the word _____. Akiko says that Ivan is right— English *is* a crazy language!

SHARING INFORMATION

Discuss these questions in pairs or small groups.

1. What country are you from?
2. What is your first language? Do you think it's a difficult language to learn? Explain your answer.
3. Do all the letters of the alphabet in your first language have only one pronunciation?
4. Did you study English in your country? If so, where and for how long?
5. Why are you studying English? Give as many reasons as you can.
6. Most jobs in the United States require English. What kinds of jobs don't require it?
7. Do you have the chance to practice English outside of class? Explain your answer.
8. Do you learn more English from class, or by using and listening to English outside of class? Explain your answer.
9. What TV programs do you watch? How much do they help you to learn English? Explain your answer.
10. Which is easier for you? To understand the English you hear or to speak English?

DICTATION

1. *Listen while the teacher reads the dialog without stopping.* <u>*Don't write anything.*</u>

2. *The teacher will read the dialog a second time, pausing after the missing lines.* <u>*Write in the missing lines.*</u>

3. *The teacher will read the dialog a third time.* <u>*Check your work.*</u>

Akiko: A second language is always difficult.

Ivan: _____

Akiko: A crazy language? Why do you say that?

Ivan: _____

Akiko: Can you give me an example?

Ivan: _____

Akiko: Hmm. They all sound different.

Ivan: _____

Akiko: No wonder English is so hard.

Ivan: _____

Where Do You Want to Go, Ma'am?

1. **hint** *n.* a suggestion that is made indirectly "I told my boyfriend there were some nice restaurants in the area. He got the <u>hint</u> and took me out to dinner."
2. **hurry** *n.* the act of moving fast "Oscar is in a <u>hurry</u>. He has a soccer game right after work."
3. **imagine** *v.* to form an idea or picture of something in one's mind "You can <u>imagine</u> how happy the President was to win reelection."
4. **ma'am** (a short form of **madam**) *n.* a polite word used in speaking to a woman "May I help you with those packages, <u>ma'am</u>?"
5. **tip** *n.* extra money given to waiters, barbers, hairdressers, and taxi drivers for their personal service "Don't forget to leave a <u>tip</u> for the waiter."
6. **tough** *adj.* difficult "Our math teacher gives <u>tough</u> tests."

PREVIEW QUESTIONS

Discuss these questions before reading the dialog.

1. Chicago is the third largest city in the United States. Where is it?
2. What kind of weather do you think Chicago has in the winter? in the summer?
3. Do you think that a taxi driver in a large city like Chicago has an interesting job? Is it dangerous? Explain your answers.

Lisa lives in Chicago. She takes a taxi to meet a friend near the Sears Tower. Her taxi driver, Ken, enjoys meeting people. Lisa and Ken talk about Chicago, its weather, and his job.

Ken: Where do you want to go, ma'am?

Lisa: Adams Street, near the Sears Tower.[1]

Ken: Are you new in Chicago?

Lisa: I came here a year and a half ago.

Ken: Do you like it here?

Lisa: Yes and no. I like the big department stores and the lake.

Ken: What don't you like?

Lisa: Everyone is always in a hurry.

Ken: You're right. And what do you think of our weather?

Lisa: Summer is nice.

Ken: And winter?

Lisa: It's too cold and windy.

Ken: That's true, and we get a lot of snow.

Lisa: We sure do! Do you like your job?

Ken: Yes, but it's tough work, and sometimes it's dangerous.

Lisa: I can imagine, but it must be interesting.

Ken: Yes, I meet a lot of interesting people.

Lisa: And you certainly enjoy talking to them.

Ken: True, and I like good tips.

Lisa: Is that a hint?

Ken: Yes, I guess it is!

---

1. The **Sears Tower** is a 110-story building in the business district of Chicago. It's the tallest building in the United States.

TRUE OR FALSE

If the sentence is true, write T. *If it's false, write* F.

_____   1. Lisa is in Chicago for a short visit.

_____   2. There are some things about Chicago that she doesn't like.

_____   3. She likes large stores that sell all kinds of things.

_____   4. She likes Chicago's winter weather.

_____   5. Ken has an easy job.

_____   6. He's shy.

_____   7. He meets a lot of interesting people.

_____   8. He indirectly asks for a good tip.

DIALOG REVIEW

Complete the paragraphs with these words.

interesting	**ago**	**tips**	**windy**	**department stores**
weather	**hint**	**hurry**	**near**	**dangerous**

Lisa tells Ken, her taxi driver, that she wants to go to Adams Street

_____ the Sears Tower.   He asks her if she's new in Chicago.

She tells him she came to the city a year and a half _____.

Ken wants to know if Lisa likes Chicago.   She tells him that she likes the lake

and the big _____.   She also says that everyone in the city is

always in a _____, which she doesn't like.

Ken asks what she thinks of Chicago's _____.   She

replies that summer is nice, but that winter is too cold and

_____.

She asks Ken if he likes his job.   He says he does, but that it's tough work and

sometimes _____.   He also says he meets a lot of

_____ people.

He tells Lisa he likes good _____.   She asks if that's a

_____.   He replies yes—he guesses it is.

SHARING INFORMATION

Discuss these questions in pairs or small groups.

1. Name some department stores.
2. Do you like to shop in department stores? Explain your answer.
3. Do you have a favorite? If so, which one?
4. How cold does it get in your country?
5. Does it snow in your country? A lot?
6. Do you like cold weather? Do you like snow? Explain your answers.
7. Do you like hot weather? Explain your answer.
8. Is it expensive to take a taxi in the United States?
9. Are taxis expensive in your country?
10. Do taxi drivers in the United States expect tips? Do people usually tip taxi drivers in your country?

STORY COMPLETION

A Waitress

Eileen is a waitress at a French restaurant. She used to work at J.C. Penney's, but didn't like it there. She doesn't live far from the restaurant and often walks to work. She likes working at the restaurant.

Complete the story with these words.

interesting	**near**	**department store**	**tips**
weather	**ago**	**in a hurry**	**tough**

Eileen is a waitress at a French restaurant. She started working there six months _____. Before that, she worked at J.C. Penney's, a large _____, but she didn't like it there. Her boss was _____, and the job wasn't very _____.

Eileen likes working in the restaurant, but she has to work fast, especially when her customers are _____.

Eileen is very pleasant, and she makes a lot of money on _____.

She lives _____ the restaurant, and she walks to work when the _____ is nice.

A Tough Teacher

WORD PREVIEW

1. **biography** *n.* the story of a person's life, written by another "I'm reading a biography of Thomas Jefferson. His life was very interesting."

2. **due** *adj.* expected to arrive by a certain time "My application to college is due in a week." "The plane is due in ten minutes."

3. **fail** *v.* to give (or receive) a grade that shows a student did not pass a test or a subject "Our science teacher failed five students."

4. **gee** *idiom* an informal word expressing surprise "Gee, it's 3:30 already."

5. **goal** *n.* what one hopes to do; an aim "Our goal is to save enough money to buy a house."

6. **main** *adj.* the most important "What is the main idea of the story?"

7. **mark** *n.* a score on a test or in a subject; a grade "Susan got a D in history; her other marks were A's and B's."

8. **oral** *adj.* spoken, not written "Our English teacher is going to give us an oral examination."

9. **summary** *n.* a shortened form of a book, chapter, story, speech, etc., giving only the most important ideas of the original "For homework, we have to write a summary of the first chapter of our history book."

10. **wrestler** *n.* a person who wrestles, who participates in the sport of wrestling (*Wrestling* is a sport in which two contestants try to throw each other to the ground.) "A wrestler has to be strong and quick."

PREVIEW QUESTIONS

Discuss these questions before reading the dialog.

1. Abraham Lincoln was the 16th President of the United States. What else do you know about him?
2. Is Lincoln popular in your country? If so, why?
3. How do you feel about doing book reports? Do you like them? Do they help you to learn? Explain your answers.

Malini, who was born in India, is reading a biography of Abraham Lincoln. She has to do a book report on Lincoln for her English teacher, Miss Johnson. It's due on Monday, and if it's late, she'll get a zero on the report. She's talking to her brother, Vijay.

Vijay:	What are you reading?
Malini:	A biography of Abraham Lincoln.
Vijay:	Is it interesting?
Malini:	Very. Did you know that Lincoln was a great wrestler?
Vijay:	You've got to be kidding!
Malini:	I'm not, and he was also the best storyteller in town.
Vijay:	The only thing I know about Lincoln is that he freed the slaves.[1]
Malini:	He also saved the Union. That was his main goal.[2]
Vijay:	Is it a long book?
Malini:	Not too long—150 pages, and it's got lots of pictures.
Vijay:	Why are you reading it?
Malini:	I have to do a book report for Miss Johnson.
Vijay:	When is it due?
Malini:	Monday. I don't have much time.
Vijay:	What if you hand it in late?
Malini:	I'll get a zero.
Vijay:	Gee, Miss Johnson is tough. And I hear she fails a lot of kids.
Malini:	That's right, and I want a good mark.
Vijay:	Do you have to give an oral report too?
Malini:	No, just written. I have to write a five-page summary of the book.
Vijay:	Good luck!
Malini:	Thanks. I need it!

1. **Lincoln** was President during the Civil War between the North and the South (1861-1865). Lincoln's Emancipation Proclamation on January 1, 1863 freed the slaves living in the 11 Southern states.
2. Lincoln's **main goal** was to save the Union, to keep the United States one country.

COMPREHENSION

Answer these questions in pairs or small groups. Use your own ideas to answer questions with an asterisk.

1. What is Malini reading?
2. What was President Lincoln's main goal?
3. Why is Malini reading a book about Lincoln?
4. What will happen if her book report is late?
*5. Do you think it's fair to give students a zero if their book reports are late? Explain your answer.
6. What kind of book report does Miss Johnson want?
*7. Do you think Malini will have her book report in on time? Explain your answer.

DIALOG REVIEW

Complete the paragraphs with these words.

zero	freed	due	fails	wrestler
mark	biography	summary	goal	tough

Malini is reading a _____ of Abraham Lincoln. She asks Vijay if he knows that Lincoln was a great _____. He doesn't.

The only thing that Vijay knows about Lincoln is that he _____ the slaves. Malini tells him that Lincoln also saved the Union, which was his main _____.

Malini is reading about Lincoln because she has to do a book report for Miss Johnson, her English teacher. It's _____ on Monday. Malini doesn't have much time, and if it's late, she'll get a _____.

Vijay says that Miss Johnson is _____, and he hears that she _____ a lot of kids. Malini knows that, and she wants a good _____.

She has to write a five-page _____ of her book.

SHARING INFORMATION

Discuss these questions in pairs or small groups.

1. Who is the President of the United States? What do you know about him?
2. Are you interested in politics? Explain your answer.
3. Name some places and things in the United States that are named after Abraham Lincoln.
4. Do you know of anything in your country that is named after Lincoln?
5. Lincoln was a great storyteller. Do you think that helped him get elected President of the United States? Explain your answer.
6. Lincoln was a very good wrestler too. Do you like wrestling? Do you ever watch it on TV?
7. Do you read much in your first language? What do you read?
8. Do you read much in English? What do you read?
9. Do you have to give book reports often? When did you give your last one? What was the book about?
10. Do you learn more when you have a tough teacher? Explain your answer.

MATCHING

Match the words in Column A with their definitions or descriptions in Column B. Print the letters on the blank lines.

Column A

_____ 1. goal

_____ 2. at least

_____ 3. summary

_____ 4. due

_____ 5. wonder (noun)

_____ 6. oral

_____ 7. wrestling

_____ 8. hint

_____ 9. biography

_____ 10. gee

_____ 11. imagine

_____ 12. mark

Column B

A. expected by a certain time

B. to picture in the mind

C. spoken

D. a minimum of

E. a suggestion made indirectly

F. idiom that expresses surprise

G. a score on a test

H. an aim

I. a sport

J. something very unusual

K. the story of someone's life

L. a shortened form of a story

Looking for a Job

1. **ad** (a short form of **advertisement**) *n.* information about a product placed in a newspaper, magazine, etc., to get people to buy the product "Sears has a big <u>ad</u> in today's newspaper."

2. **although** *conj.* in contrast to the fact that; in spite of the fact that "<u>Although</u> Julie doesn't feel well, she's going to the party."

3. **at first** *idiom* in the beginning "<u>At first</u>, Bret didn't like college, but now he loves it."

4. **cashier** *n.* the person in a store who takes one's money for the things one buys "I gave the <u>cashier</u> $50, and she gave me $10 in change."

5. **employment agency** *n.* an agency that tries to find jobs for people "The <u>employment agency</u> helped Donna get a good job."

6. **experience** *n.* the knowledge and ability that come from doing something "Regina has a lot of <u>experience</u> with computers."

7. **fill out** *v.* to write answers to questions on a form (*Form* is explained below.) "The doctor asked me to <u>fill out</u> a form before he examined me."

8. **form** *n.* a printed paper with questions and blank spaces for answers "Before you talk to Mrs. Morales about the job, you have to answer the questions on this <u>form</u>."

9. **miss** *v.* to feel unhappy because someone you love is not with you "Our son is away at college, and we <u>miss</u> him very much."

10. **operate** *v.* to use; to run "It's easy to <u>operate</u> a copying machine."

11. **quickly** *adv.* fast "Chris is almost finished. He works <u>quickly</u>."

12. **require** *v.* to need "A baby <u>requires</u> a lot of love and care."

13. **sewing machine** *n.* a machine that uses a needle and thread to repair or make clothing "My grandmother made many of her own dresses on a <u>sewing machine</u>."

14. **unemployment compensation** *n.* money given to workers who have lost their jobs "Joyce isn't working, but she's getting <u>unemployment compensation</u>."

PREVIEW QUESTIONS

Discuss these questions before reading the story.

1. When did you come to the United States?
2. How did you feel when you first came?
3. Where are the other members of your family? In the United States or in your country?

Kristina Rakowski was born in Warsaw, the capital of Poland. She came to the United States five years ago. She was only 17. Her mother and father stayed in Poland, so Kristina went to live with her aunt and cousins. Life in the United States wasn't easy for Kristina. Although her aunt and cousins were nice to her, she missed her parents, friends, and country, and had to work very hard.

At first, Kristina worked in a factory near her house. She was good at operating a sewing machine, and she got a job quickly. Unfortunately, the factory closed, and Kristina lost her job. After that, she collected unemployment compensation.

Kristina began to look for a new job. She went to the state employment agency and filled out a form. However, the employment agency wasn't able to place[1] her. Every day she read the help-wanted ads[2] in the newspaper. She told her friends that she was looking for a job. The problem was that most jobs required experience, and she had very little.

Kristina finally got a job as a cashier at Foodtown, a supermarket near her house. The pay wasn't great, but it was nicer than working in a factory, and she was able to walk to work. At first, she liked her new job. It was different. After a few months, however, the job became boring. There was no future in being a cashier.

---

1. In this sentence, **place** means *to find a job for*. "Colleges try to place their graduates in good jobs."
2. A **help-wanted ad** is an advertisement that gives information about a job so that people will apply for it. *Help-wanted ads* are placed in a special section of the newspaper. "Phil is looking for a job. That's why he reads the help-wanted ads every day."

TRUE OR FALSE

If the sentence is true, write T. *If it's false, write* F.

_____ 1. Kristina's mother and father came to the United States with her.

_____ 2. For a long time, Kristina couldn't find a job in the United States.

_____ 3. She was able to sew, and that helped her get her first job.

_____ 4. She lost her job when the factory closed.

_____ 5. She continued to receive money after she lost her job.

_____ 6. The state employment agency got her a new job.

_____ 7. She read the newspaper and talked to friends to find another job.

_____ 8. She never liked her job as a cashier.

STORY COMPLETION

Joining the Marines

Hakeem is 18 and is applying to the Marines. He knows it'll be hard to leave his family and friends, but he wants to be a Marine.   He also has to pass a physical exam, but that won't be hard.   He's strong and healthy.

Complete the story with these words.

miss	**filling out**	**require**	**quickly**
however	**at first**	**began**	**although**

_____ he's only 18, Hakeem is _____ an application for the United States Marines.

He _____ to think about joining the Marines in September of his senior year in high school and _____ decided he wanted to be a Marine.

Hakeem knows he will _____ his family and friends, especially _____ , but he still wants to be a Marine.

The Marines _____ a high-school diploma and a physical exam. _____ , that's no problem. Hakeem graduated from high school in June and is strong and healthy.

SHARING INFORMATION

Discuss these questions in pairs or small groups. Space is provided to write your answers if you wish.

1. Are you working? If so, what do you do?

    _____

    _____

2. Where do you work? What hours do you work?

    _____

    _____

3. Do you like your job? Why or why not?

    _____

    _____

4. Is it easy to get a job in the United States? Explain your answer.

    _____

    _____

5. It it easy to get a job in your country? Explain your answer.

    _____

    _____

6. How can friends sometimes help a person get a job?

    _____

    _____

7. Look at the help-wanted ads in the newspaper, and bring to class one that you find interesting. On the lines below, write what the ad says.

    _____

    _____

8. Kristina felt there was no future in being a cashier. Why do you think she felt that way?

    _____

    _____

Good Tips and High Hopes

1. **apply** *v.* to ask for something formally and in writing, for example, to ask to be accepted into a college "Dennis is applying for a credit card."
2. **bank account** *n.* a sum of money kept in a bank "How much money do you have in your bank account?"
3. **beautician** *n.* a person who cares for people's hair, skin, and nails "I like the way my beautician does my hair."
4. **beauty salon** *n.* a place of business where people have their hair, skin, and nails cared for "Linda is going to the beauty salon to have her hair and nails done."
5. **customer** *n.* a person who buys something "If we want to stay in business, we have to keep our customers happy."
6. **diploma** *n.* an official paper stating that a person graduated from a high school, college, or other school "Reggie showed me his high-school diploma."
7. **far** *adv.* at a great distance "New York City is far from Los Angeles."
8. **government** *n.* the people and system that rule a country or state "Taxes are high because the government spends a lot of money."
9. **grant** *n.* money given by the government to help pay for one's education "Jason's family doesn't have much money, but he's going to college with the help of a grant."
10. **grow** *v.* to become bigger "Our business is small, but it's growing."
11. **interview** *n.* a formal meeting in which a person who is applying for a job or to a college is asked questions "Robert went for a job interview this morning."
12. **license** *n.* legal permission to do something, for example, a license to fish "You need a license to hunt."
13. **pass** *v.* to get a satisfactory mark on an exam "Did you pass the biology exam?"
14. **training** *n.* instruction and practice in how to do something "Dawn knows a lot about computers, but she wants more training."
15. **tuition** *n.* the money that a school charges for the instruction it gives "The tuition at private colleges is high."
16. **yellow pages** *n.* the section of the phone book that lists all kinds of businesses and is printed on yellow paper "I'm looking in the yellow pages to find a good place to rent a car."

PREVIEW QUESTIONS

Discuss these questions before reading the story.

1. Do you think beauticians have a good job? Is their work interesting?
2. Do they work hard? Do they make good money?
3. Do you need a license to work as a beautician? If so, why?

One day Kristina decided to become a beautician. She looked in the yellow pages of the phone book and found the name of a beauty school[1] not too far from her house. She went there for an interview. The school accepted Kristina, and she applied for a government grant to help pay her tuition. She received the grant, but continued to work at Foodtown because she needed the money.

Kristina liked beauty school, but it was difficult because she knew very little English. She brought a dictionary to class, and the other students helped her. One of them knew Polish. To obtain her diploma, she had to attend school for 1,200 hours. The classes and training were interesting, and she learned a lot. Kristina also made many new friends.

After she finished school, Kristina had to take an exam to obtain her license to be a beautician. The exam was long and hard, and she was a little nervous. However, she was a good student and she passed.

Now Kristina is working at a busy beauty salon two blocks from her school. Her salary isn't big, but she's getting good experience, and she makes a lot of money on tips. Her customers tip her well because she's friendly and does a good job. She saves as much money as she can, and her bank account is growing. Kristina works hard and is ambitious. Some day she hopes to have her own beauty salon.

---

1. A **beauty school** teaches its students how to care for and treat people's hair, skin, and nails. It prepares its students to become licensed beauticians.

COMPREHENSION

Answer these questions in pairs or small groups. Use your own ideas to answer questions with an asterisk.

1. After she was accepted to beauty school, what did Kristina apply for? Why?
2. Why did she continue to work at Foodtown?
3. Why was beauty school difficult for Kristina?
4. What did she have to do to obtain her diploma?
5. What did she have to take after she finished school?
6. Why do her customers tip her well?
*7. Do you think Kristina likes being a beautician? Explain your answer.
*8. Do you think she will have her own beauty salon some day? Explain your answer.

STORY COMPLETION

Going to Law School

Leslie wants to be a lawyer. She did well on the law-school entrance exam and is going to visit a law school tomorrow. She has some money in the bank, but she's also going to need a loan to go to law school.

Complete the story with these words.

beauty salon	**ambitious**	**although**	**tuition**
applying	**account**	**interview**	**passed**

Leslie is going to graduate from college in two months. She's _____ and very smart and wants to be a lawyer. She easily _____ the law-school entrance exam.

Leslie is _____ to three law schools and has an _____ at one of them tomorrow afternoon. Tomorrow morning she's going to the _____ so that she'll look her best.

_____ Leslie has some money in her savings _____, she's going to need a loan to help pay her _____ and other expenses at law school.

SHARING INFORMATION

Discuss these questions in pairs or small groups. Space is provided to write your answers if you wish.

1. What is an education grant? Who gives grants?

    _____

    _____

2. Does receiving a grant usually depend on financial need or one's grades in school?

    _____

    _____

3. What is the difference between a grant and a loan?

    _____

    _____

4. Kristina brought a dictionary to class. Do you use a bilingual dictionary? Do you use it often? Does it help much?

    _____

    _____

5. Kristina is ambitious. Do you have an ambition in life—something you want to do or be very much? If so, what is it?

    _____

    _____

6. Kristina wants to have her own business some day. Do you? If so, what kind of business?

    _____

    _____

7. What are some of the advantages of owning your own business?

    _____

    _____

8. What are some of the disadvantages?

    _____

    _____

SYNONYMS

Synonyms are words that have the same or a similar meaning. In the blank spaces, write a synonym for the underlined word or words.

just	grow	crazy	hurry	a tip
tough	save	stay	quickly	main

1. That's a <u>difficult</u> question. _____
2. You're <u>foolish</u> to leave all that money in your room. _____
3. I don't have a driver's license. I'm <u>only</u> 15. _____
4. I'm sorry, but we have to leave. We're in a <u>rush</u>. _____
5. Vladimir decided to <u>remain</u> in Russia. _____
6. What's the company's <u>biggest</u> problem? _____
7. I'm going to <u>keep</u> this magazine. _____
8. We always give the barber <u>extra money</u>. _____
9. My new computer works <u>fast</u>. _____
10. Your plants will <u>get bigger</u>. _____

ANTONYMS

Antonyms are words that have opposite meanings. In the blank spaces, write an antonym for each word.

pass	long	best	be born	however
future	close	dangerous	far	accept

1. worst _____
2. fail _____
3. near _____
4. short _____
5. past _____
6. therefore _____
7. safe _____
8. reject _____
9. open _____
10. die _____

6

COUPLES AND HOUSING

No Kiss This Morning?

WORD PREVIEW

1. **as . . . as** *conj.* to the same degree that "Jamal is <u>as</u> tall <u>as</u> his brother."
2. **briefcase** *n.* a small, flat case used to carry papers, books, pens, and similar items (*Briefcase* is a combination of the words *brief* and *case*.) "I have an extra pen and a notebook in my <u>briefcase</u>."
3. **had better** *idiom* should; have to "It's starting to rain. You <u>had better</u> take an umbrella."

PREVIEW QUESTIONS

Discuss these questions before reading the dialog.

1. Do you know people who always seem to forget where they put things?
2. Are you good at remembering where you put things?
3. Do you usually leave for school or work at the last minute, so that you have to rush to be on time?

Jeff has to leave his house by 8:30 to get to work on time. Every morning he's rushing at the last minute. He also forgets where he puts things. Fortunately, his wife, Sara, has a good memory.

Sara:	It's getting late, Jeff.
Jeff:	What time is it?
Sara:	Ten after eight.[1]
Jeff:	Where's my new brown shirt?
Sara:	In the bedroom closet, dear. Where else would it be?
Jeff:	Did you see my briefcase?
Sara:	It's on the dining room table where you left it.
Jeff:	You never forget where you put things.
Sara:	Sometimes I do, but I'm not as bad as you.
Jeff:	What are you having for breakfast?
Sara:	Orange juice, coffee, and toast.
Jeff:	I don't have time for breakfast.
Sara:	Then at least have a cup of coffee.
Jeff:	Thanks, dear . . . The coffee tastes good.

(20 minutes later)

Sara:	It's 8:30.
Jeff:	I've got five minutes to catch my bus.
Sara:	You had better hurry.
Jeff:	Where are my glasses?
Sara:	On top of the TV.
Jeff:	OK. Good-bye, honey.
Sara:	No kiss this morning?
Jeff:	Of course! I always kiss you before I leave.
Sara:	I know, but some day you'll forget that too!

---

1. **Ten after eight.** = Ten minutes after eight.   We often indicate time by giving the number of minutes after the hour.   "It's twenty after ten."

COMPREHENSION

Answer these questions in pairs or small groups. Use your own ideas to answer questions with an asterisk.

1. Where's Jeff's new brown shirt?
2. Where did he leave his briefcase?
3. What is Sara having for breakfast?
4. Why doesn't Jeff have more than a cup of coffee for breakfast?
5. How much time does he have to catch his bus?
*6. Do you think Sara is patient? Explain your answer.
*7. Do you think Jeff depends too much on his wife? Explain your answer.

DIALOG REVIEW

Complete the paragraphs with these words.

left	breakfast	on top of	tastes	briefcase
catch	closet	forgets	had better	as bad as

It's getting late, and Jeff is looking for his new brown shirt. It's in the bedroom _____ .

Now he can't find his _____ . His wife, Sara, tells him it's on the dining room table where he _____ it.

Sometimes Sara also _____ where she puts things, but she's not _____ Jeff.

Sara has orange juice, coffee, and toast for _____ . Jeff has a cup of coffee. It _____ good.

Jeff's got five minutes to _____ his bus. Sara tells him he _____ hurry, but he can't find his glasses. They're _____ the TV.

Jeff kisses his wife good-bye, but she says that some day he'll forget that too!

SHARING INFORMATION

Discuss these questions in pairs or small groups.

1. What time do you usually get up in the morning?
2. Most people hate to get up in the morning. Do you?
3. Like Jeff, many people eat very little for breakfast. Why?
4. What do you usually have for breakfast?
5. What do people usually eat for breakfast in your country?
6. What time do you leave home for work or school?
7. How do you get to work or school?
8. How long does it take?
9. How often are you late to work or school?
   (a) frequently   (b) sometimes   (c) almost never   (d) never
10. Are you understanding of people who are late and make you wait, or do you get impatient (impatient = not patient)?

DICTATION

1. *Listen while the teacher reads the dialog without stopping.* <u>*Don't write anything*</u>.

2. *The teacher will read the dialog a second time, pausing after the missing lines.* <u>*Write in the missing lines*</u>.

3. *The teacher will read the dialog a third time.* <u>*Check your work*</u>.

Jeff:	Where's my new brown shirt?
Sara:	_____
Jeff:	Did you see my briefcase?
Sara:	_____
Jeff:	You never forget where you put things.
Sara:	_____
Jeff:	What are you having for breakfast?
Sara:	_____
Jeff:	I don't have time for breakfast.
Sara:	_____
Jeff:	Thanks, dear . . . The coffee tastes good.

A Mouse in the Kitchen

1. **argue** *v.* to fight with words; to disagree "If I say *yes,* Jane says *no.* If I say *no,* she says *yes.* She loves to <u>argue</u>."
2. **either** *adv.* also (used in negative sentences) "Scott doesn't want to go to the dance, and I don't <u>either</u>."
3. **horrible** *adj.* very bad; very unpleasant "We'll never go to that restaurant again. The food was <u>horrible</u>."
4. **mousetrap** *n.* a device to capture and kill a mouse (A *trap* is a device to capture an animal. *Mousetrap* is a combination of the words *mouse* and *trap.*) "Fred saw a mouse in his basement. He's going to the store to buy some <u>mousetraps</u>."
5. **set** *v.* to put something in a position so that it will work "Connie <u>set</u> her alarm for seven o'clock."
6. **So what?** *idiom* Who cares?; I don't care. "If you don't give me my bike, I'm going to tell Mom." "<u>So what?</u> I don't care."

116

PREVIEW QUESTIONS

Discuss these questions before reading the dialog.

1. Why are so many people afraid of mice?[1]
2. Do you know anyone who is afraid of them?
3. Are you?

Karen sees a mouse in the kitchen. She's afraid of mice. She calls her husband, Dick, and he comes to the kitchen. Dick gets some cheese, and Karen gets a mousetrap. She sets the trap and puts it next to the refrigerator.

Karen:	Help! Help! Dick, come here!
Dick:	What's wrong, Karen?
Karen:	There's a mouse in the kitchen.
Dick:	Are you sure?
Karen:	Of course, I am! I saw it.
Dick:	Are you afraid of a little mouse?
Karen:	You know I am. I hate mice. And you don't like them either.
Dick:	True, but I'm not *afraid* of them.
Karen:	So what? You're afraid of dogs, and I'm not.
Dick:	That's different. Dogs can bite.
Karen:	It's not different. Besides, most dogs are friendly. Mice are horrible!
Dick:	Let's not argue. Is there a mousetrap in the house?
Karen:	Yes, there's one in the kitchen cabinet.
Dick:	And there's some cheese in the refrigerator. I'll get it.
Karen:	Good. I'll get the mousetrap.
Dick:	Here's the cheese.
Karen:	I have the trap. I'll set it.
Dick:	Be careful, Karen. Watch[2] your fingers!
Karen:	Don't worry. The trap is set. Where shall we put it?
Dick:	Next to the refrigerator. Poor mouse!

---

1. The plural of **mouse** is *mice*.
2. **Watch** often means *look at*. "Katie is watching TV." However, in the dialog *watch* means *be careful of*. "Watch your fingers!" = "Be careful of your fingers!"

TRUE OR FALSE

If the sentence is true, write T. *If it's false, write* F.

_____   1. Karen shouts for help when she sees a mouse.

_____   2. Dick doesn't like mice.

_____   3. He's afraid of them.

_____   4. Karen is afraid of dogs.

_____   5. There's a mousetrap in the kitchen cabinet.

_____   6. Dick is afraid that Karen may get hurt setting the trap.

_____   7. Dick sets the trap.

_____   8. He and Karen decide to put the trap behind the refrigerator.

DIALOG REVIEW

Complete the paragraphs with these words.

bite	next to	hates	argue	watch
set	horrible	one	worry	either

Karen sees a mouse in the kitchen. She calls her husband, Dick. He asks Karen if she's afraid of a little mouse. She is. She _____ mice, and he doesn't like them _____, but he's not afraid of them.

Dick, however, is afraid of dogs, and Karen isn't. He says a fear of dogs is different because they can _____. She says it's not different and that most dogs are friendly, but mice are _____.

Dick doesn't want to _____. He asks if there is a mousetrap in the house. There's _____ in the kitchen cabinet and some cheese in the refrigerator.

Karen gets the trap and says she'll _____ it. Dick tells her to _____ her fingers. She tells him not to _____.

She puts the trap _____ the refrigerator.

SHARING INFORMATION

Discuss these questions in pairs or small groups.

1. What problems can mice cause?
2. Karen thinks mice are horrible. Some people think they're cute. What do you think?
3. Why are mice so useful in the field of medicine?
4. What is the difference between a mouse and a rat?
5. Did you ever set a mousetrap? Was it easy?
6. Why are mousetraps dangerous?
7. Are you afraid of dogs?
8. Do you think most dogs are friendly?
9. Did a dog ever bite you? If so, tell us about it.
10. Name some things people are afraid of besides mice and dogs?

STORY COMPLETION

A Dog, a Cat, and a Snake

Mr. Steinberg and I are neighbors and good friends. He has a dog, a cat, and a pet snake. I like the dog and the cat, but not the snake.

Complete the story with these words.

argue	**besides**	**horrible**	**bite**
afraid of	**next to**	**careful**	**wrong**

Mr. Steinberg lives in a large house _____ the park. We're neighbors and good friends, and we never _____ .

Mr. Steinberg has a big dog named Happy. Happy is friendly and doesn't _____ . I like him. _____ Happy, Mr. Steinberg has a cat and a pet snake.

Now there's nothing _____ with having a dog and a cat, but I think his snake is _____ , and I'm _____ it. That's why I'm _____ to stay away from it.

It's a Deal

1. **already** *adv.* by or before this time   "The clothes are dry <u>already</u>."
2. **cushion** *n.* the part of a living room chair that we sit on (It's made of soft material and has a cover.)   "I love these <u>cushions</u>. They're so soft and comfortable."
3. **deal** *n.* an agreement between two people (or groups) that is good for both   "Tracy made a <u>deal</u> with her boss. She's going to leave an hour early today and work an extra hour tomorrow."
4. **excited** *adj.* having strong feelings; not calm   "Jonathan is <u>excited</u> about going to the concert."
5. **hey** *idiom* an informal word used to express surprise or happiness, or to get someone's attention   "<u>Hey</u>, I got a letter from my cousin." "<u>Hey</u>, Larry, look at these pictures."
6. **ignition** *n.* the electrical system that starts the motor of a car   "You have to put the key in the <u>ignition</u> and turn it to start the car."
7. **so** *conj.* with the purpose that; in order that   "Andy is studying hard <u>so</u> he can get good grades."
8. **stand** *v.* to tolerate; to accept (something unpleasant)   "I can't <u>stand</u> the heat in my apartment. I'm going to buy an air conditioner."

PREVIEW QUESTIONS

Discuss these questions before reading the dialog.

1. Do you frequently lose or misplace things? If not, do you know anyone who does?
2. Do you watch TV every day? For how long?
3. Do you ever watch football games on TV? How often?

Terry loses her car keys and looks everywhere for them. After she finds them, she asks her husband to go shopping with her. However, he wants to watch a football game on TV.

Terry:	Did you see my car keys?
Dave:	No, I didn't.
Terry:	I wonder where they are.
Dave:	Did you look in your coat?
Terry:	Yes, I did. They're not in my coat or my handbag.
Dave:	Don't worry. You'll find them.
Terry:	But I've looked everywhere. I can't stand to lose things!
Dave:	Maybe the keys are still in the ignition.
Terry:	No, I already checked the car.
Dave:	Did you check the sofa? Look under the cushions.
Terry:	That's a good idea . . . Hey, you're right! Here they are!
Dave:	Great! Now you can go shopping.
Terry:	You're coming with me, aren't you?[1]
Dave:	No, dear. There's a big football game on TV.
Terry:	Not another football game on TV! That's all you do on the weekends.
Dave:	Don't get excited. I have a plan.
Terry:	I'm listening.
Dave:	Let's eat out tonight and go shopping tomorrow.
Terry:	So you can watch a game on TV?
Dave:	Yes, and so we can enjoy dinner at a nice restaurant.
Terry:	It's a deal. I love to eat out!

1. The addition of **aren't you** changes this sentence into a question. Terry expects Dave to say *yes*, but he says *no*.

COMPREHENSION

Answer these questions in pairs or small groups. Use your own ideas to answer questions with an asterisk.

1. What did Terry lose?
2. Name three places where she looked for her keys.
3. Where does she find them?
4. Dave doesn't want to go shopping. Why not?
*5. Do you think he watches too much football on TV? Explain your answer.
6. What deal does Terry accept?
*7. Why do you think she likes to eat out?

DIALOG REVIEW

Complete the paragraphs with these words.

enjoy	ignition	excited	cushions	handbag
already	deal	wonders	stand	weekends

Terry can't find her car keys. She _____ where she put them. She looks in her coat and her _____, but they're not there. Her husband, Dave, tells her not to worry, and says that she'll find them. Terry says she's looked everywhere and that she can't _____ to lose things.

Dave thinks the keys may still be in the _____, but Terry _____ checked the car. Then he tells her to look under the _____ of the sofa, and that's where she finds them.

Terry wants Dave to go shopping with her, but he wants to watch a big football game on TV. She says that the only thing he does on the _____ is watch football games on TV.

Dave tells her not to get _____. He has a plan. They can go out for dinner tonight and go shopping tomorrow. In this way, he can watch the football game, and they can _____ dinner at a nice restaurant. Terry says it's a _____. She loves to eat out.

SHARING INFORMATION

Discuss these questions in pairs or small groups.

1. Do you like to shop? Explain your answer.
2. When do you usually go shopping?
3. Do you usually shop alone or with someone? Who do you shop with?
4. Do husbands and wives in the United States frequently shop together? Do husbands and wives in your country?
5. Where do you shop for food?
6. Where do you shop for clothing? for other things?
7. Did you ever lose anything that was valuable? What? Did you ever find it?
8. Do you get very upset when you can't find what you're looking for?
9. Do you like to eat in restaurants? If so, why?
10. How often do you eat out?

MATCHING

Match the words in Column A with their definitions or descriptions in Column B. Print the letters on the blank lines.

Column A		**Column B**	
_____	1. briefcase	A.	it starts a car
_____	2. argue	B.	part of a sofa
_____	3. either	C.	to put one's teeth into
_____	4. ignition	D.	with the purpose that
_____	5. bite	E.	used to capture animals
_____	6. So what?	F.	good for carrying papers
_____	7. trap	G.	we say it to get one's attention
_____	8. set	H.	also (used in negative sentences)
_____	9. cushions	I.	a way to say "I don't care!"
_____	10. hey	J.	to tolerate
_____	11. stand	K.	to fight with words
_____	12. so	L.	to put in a position to work

The Roaches Are Back

1. **complaint** *n.* a statement saying that something is bad or wrong "The police received several <u>complaints</u> about the noise at the party."
2. **due** *adj.* the day on which a baby is expected to be born "When is the baby <u>due</u>?"
3. **exterminator** *n.* a person who kills mice or insects in a building by spraying it "The <u>exterminator</u> comes every month to spray our office."
4. **get rid of** *idiom* to become free of something one doesn't want "Brad can't <u>get rid of</u> his cold."
5. **improve** *v.* to become better "Our band played very well today. We're <u>improving</u>."
6. **lack** *n.* the absence of something one needs "A <u>lack</u> of time kept me from finishing the report."
7. **neighborhood** *n.* a small area of a city or town "Don't worry. This is a very safe <u>neighborhood</u>."
8. **pregnant** *adj.* carrying an unborn baby in the womb "Helen is <u>pregnant</u>, and her baby is due in May."
9. **rent** *n.* the money you pay to live in an apartment or to use an office "This is a very nice apartment. How much is the <u>rent</u>?"
10. **roach** (a short form of **cockroach**) *n.* an insect with a flat, brown body that lives in some buildings, especially old ones "It's an old building, and it has a lot of <u>roaches</u>."
11. **such** *adj.* of this type "It's going to be very hot today. <u>Such</u> heat is common this time of year."
12. **tiny** *adj.* very small "I'm going to have a <u>tiny</u> piece of cake. I'm on a diet."
13. **while** *n.* a period of time, especially a short one "Dinner isn't ready yet. We'll have to wait a little <u>while</u> to eat."

PREVIEW QUESTIONS

Discuss these questions before reading the story.

1. Do you rent the apartment or house in which you live?
2. Are you happy with it? If not, why not?
3. Do you get enough heat in the winter?

Nancy and Victor live in New York City, on the Lower East Side[1] of Manhattan.[2]   They got married a year ago.   The building they live in is very old, and they're unhappy about their apartment.   During the winter, they frequently call to complain about a lack of heat.   (New York and many large cities have a special phone number for such complaints.)   For a while, the situation improves, but in a few weeks the apartment is cold again.

Nancy and Victor keep their apartment neat and clean.   However, they have roaches, and they can't get rid of them.   The exterminator comes one day, but two days later the roaches are back.   Nancy and Victor hate roaches.

Their kitchen and bathroom are very small, and there is only one bedroom with a tiny closet.   The rents in the building are controlled by the city, so their rent is low.   Nancy and Victor pay only $400 a month in rent.

Victor has lived on the Lower East Side for seven years.   He and Nancy have many good friends in the neighborhood.   "We don't want to move away from our friends," Victor says.   "But there are too many problems with our apartment.   Besides, Nancy is pregnant.   The baby is due in three months, and we'll need more room. We have to move."

1. The **Lower East Side** is a section of Manhattan below 14th Street where many immigrants live. "A hundred years ago, many people came from Italy to live on the Lower East Side."
2. **Manhattan** is one of the five boroughs or divisions of New York City. It is an island with a population of over 1,400,000. "Manhattan is famous for its tall buildings, theaters, department stores, and other businesses."

TRUE OR FALSE

If the sentence is true, write T. *If it's false, write* F.

_____   1. Nancy and Victor don't like their apartment.

_____   2. There's nothing they can do about the lack of heat.

_____   3. Their apartment has roaches because it's dirty.

_____   4. Their apartment is large.

_____   5. Their rent is high.

_____   6. They like many of their neighbors.

_____   7. Nancy is going to have a baby.

_____   8. They feel they have to move.

STORY COMPLETION

Pam Isn't Like Her Mother

Mrs. Carter lives in a large house and works very hard to keep it clean. However, her daughter, Pam, doesn't like to clean her room, and it usually looks terrible.

Complete the story with these words.

tiny	complains	neat	hates
while	neighborhood	improves	gets rid of

Mrs. Carter lives in a large house in a beautiful _____ .

She's very _____ and _____ anything

she doesn't need. If she sees a _____ piece of paper on the

floor, she picks it up.

Mrs. Carter's daughter, Pam, isn't at all like her mother.   Pam

_____ to clean her room, and it looks terrible.

When her mother _____ , Pam cleans her room, and

this _____ it a lot. For a _____ , Pam's

room looks great, but in a couple of weeks it's worse than ever.

SHARING INFORMATION

Discuss these questions in pairs or small groups. Space is provided to write your answers if you wish.

1. If you have no heat or other problems with your apartment, who do you call? Or what do you?

   _____

   _____

2. What can people do to get rid of roaches? Is it easy to get rid of them?

   _____

   _____

3. Do you think your rent is fair? Or is it too high?

   _____

   _____

4. Many cities in the United States limit rent increases. This is called "rent control." Does the city in which you live have rent control?

   _____

   _____

5. Do you have enough room in the house or apartment in which you live?

   _____

   _____

6. Are you thinking about moving? If so, why?

   _____

   _____

7. How well do you know your neighbors?

   _____

   _____

8. Did you ever move from a neighborhood where you had many friends? Did you miss them? Explain your answer.

   _____

   _____

A Bargain and a Bribe

1. **afford** *v.* to be able to pay for   "Jay is rich. He can <u>afford</u> an expensive car."
2. **agree** *v.* to have the same opinion   "Natasha and I are good friends, but we don't always <u>agree</u>."
3. **bargain** *n.* an item for sale at less than the usual price   "My new suit was a <u>bargain</u>. It cost only $99."
4. **both** *pronoun* the one and the other; the two   "We had a math and a history test today, and <u>both</u> were hard."
5. **bribe** *n.* money given to get a person to do something, especially something wrong   "The company offered the mayor a <u>bribe</u> to get a contract with the city."
6. **calm down** *v.* to become calm; to become peaceful   "At first, Mr. Gallo was very angry at me, but then he <u>calmed down</u>."
7. **damage** *v.* to harm something; to make something less valuable   "The cold weather <u>damaged</u> our tomato plants."
8. **empty** *adj.* containing nothing   "There's nothing in the desk. It's <u>empty</u>."
9. **fee** *n.* money one pays for a professional service   "What was the lawyer's <u>fee</u>?"
10. **get back** *v.* to obtain again what one gave   "Virginia returned the camera to the store and <u>got</u> her money <u>back</u>."
11. **in addition** *idiom* also; besides   "Joe has a lot of homework. <u>In addition</u>, he has to go to baseball practice."
12. **in advance** *idiom* given before a certain time   "We have to pay for the plane tickets <u>in advance</u>."
13. **really** *adv.* in fact; actually   "Are you <u>really</u> going to move to San Francisco?"
14. **security deposit** *n.* money given in advance by a person who rents an apartment to pay for any damage that might be done to the apartment   "I had to pay a <u>security deposit</u> when I rented my apartment."
15. **super** (a short form of **superintendent**) *n.* a person who takes care of a building   "The <u>super</u> cleans the halls every week."

PREVIEW QUESTIONS

Discuss these questions before reading the story.

1. How did you find out about your house or apartment? From a friend? From the newspaper? In some other way?
2. If you're renting, did you have to pay a security deposit?
3. What do you think of your neighborhood? Is it quiet or noisy? Is it safe or dangerous?

Nancy and Victor want to stay in New York City. They're looking for an apartment in the Bronx.[1] They can afford to pay about $800 a month. A friend tells them about an empty apartment in a building in a quiet neighborhood. They visit the building, and the super shows them the apartment.

It's just what they want. There are two bedrooms, a nice kitchen, and a large living room. The floors are beautiful. The rent is $850 a month and includes heat and hot water, which is a bargain. The building has a small elevator. It's not modern, but it works fine.

They must pay the first month's rent and a security deposit of $850 in advance. If they don't damage the apartment, they'll get the security deposit back when they move.

In addition, the super mentions a special fee of $300 to be paid in cash. "This money is for the extra work I do in preparing and showing people the apartment," he says. "If you pay it, you'll get the apartment. If you don't, the apartment may go to someone else." Victor is angry about the special fee. He says it's really a bribe. Nancy is also upset, but they want the apartment very much. Victor calms down, and they both agree to pay the extra money. They don't want to stay in their old apartment, and they'll need more room for the baby.

---

1. The **Bronx** is one of the five boroughs or divisions of New York City. "One of the largest and best zoos in the world is in the Bronx."

COMPREHENSION

Answer these questions in pairs or small groups. Use your own ideas to answer questions with an asterisk.

1. How much rent can Nancy and Victor afford to pay?
2. Describe the kitchen, living room, and floors of the apartment they're looking at.
3. Describe the elevator in the apartment building.
4. How much do they have to pay in advance?
5. What happens to the security deposit if they don't damage the apartment?
*6. Do you think the security deposit is a good idea? Explain your answer.
7. What reason does the super give for the special fee?
*8. Do you think this fee is fair, or is it really a bribe? Explain your answer.

STORY COMPLETION

Going to Hawaii

Todd and Shannon are planning to go to Hawaii for their vacation. It'll be expensive, but they have the money. Besides, a travel agency is offering them a good price.

Complete the story with these words.

fees	both	cash	afford
in addition	agree	bargain	in advance

Todd and Shannon want to go to Hawaii for a week. It won't be cheap, but they're _____ working and they can _____ it. _____, a travel agency is offering them a price that's a _____.

The price includes all _____ and expenses, except for meals.

They can pay by _____ or use their credit card, but they must pay _____. Todd and Shannon _____ to use their credit card.

SHARING INFORMATION

Discuss these questions in pairs or small groups. Space is provided to write your answers if you wish.

1. Did you rent a house or an apartment in your country? Are rents high there?

   _____

   _____

2. Is a security deposit required when you rent an apartment or a house in your country?

   _____

   _____

3. Do you have a super in the building in which you live? If so, what does the super do?

   _____

   _____

4. Do the super and the owner take good care of the building?

   _____

   _____

5. When a person plans to rent an apartment or buy a house, how important is the neighborhood? Explain your answer.

   _____

   _____

6. What are some of the advantages of living in a big city like New York?

   _____

   _____

7. What are some of the disadvantages?

   _____

   _____

8. Would you like to live in New York City? Explain your answer.

   _____

   _____

SYNONYMS

Synonyms are words that have the same or a similar meaning. In the blank spaces, write a synonym for the underlined word or words.

fee	improve	already	check	besides
deal	just	had better	pregnant	afford

1. What do you think of the <u>agreement</u> between the two companies?
    _____

2. The bank has closed <u>by this time</u>. _____

3. I'm not getting that coat. It's too expensive. <u>In addition</u>, I don't like the color. _____

4. You look tired. You <u>should</u> get some rest. _____

5. There's a small <u>charge</u> to enter the museum. _____

6. Yvette is <u>expecting a baby</u>. _____

7. Matt looks <u>exactly</u> like his father. _____

8. The dentist is going to <u>examine</u> my teeth. _____

9. I want to buy that computer, but I can't <u>pay for</u> it. _____

10. If our team practices more, we'll <u>do better</u>. _____

ANTONYMS

Antonyms are words that have opposite meanings. In the blank spaces, write an antonym for each word.

empty	in advance	on top of	special	quiet
calm down	wrong	get rid of	tiny	horrible

1. acquire _____
2. noisy _____
3. full _____
4. large _____
5. right _____
6. very good _____
7. under _____
8. get excited _____
9. ordinary _____
10. afterwards _____

7

CARS
AND
TRAVEL

I Want to Learn to Drive

WORD PREVIEW

1. **come on** *idiom* please "<u>Come on</u>, Mom! Let me go to the movies." "<u>Come on</u>. Tell me what happened." (See page 68, Word Preview, for a different meaning of *come on*.)

2. **expensive** *adj.* costing a lot of money "We like the car very much, but we're not going to buy it. It's too <u>expensive</u>."

3. **flatter** *v.* to praise a person insincerely, usually to win favor "I hate the way Doug is always <u>flattering</u> the boss."

4. **go ahead** *idiom* to begin or continue to do something "That's a good idea. <u>Go ahead</u> with it."

5. **mean** *adj.* unkind; not willing to help "Heather won't let the other children play with her new toys. That's <u>mean</u>."

6. **patience** *n.* the ability to accept calmly what one doesn't like; the ability to wait calmly "Ted loses his <u>patience</u> when he has to wait in line."

7. **permit** *n.* a paper or card saying that one has the permission to do something "You can't park here without a <u>permit</u>."

8. **terrific** *adj.* very good "Denise is a <u>terrific</u> cook."

PREVIEW QUESTIONS

Discuss these questions before reading the dialog.

1. Can you drive? Do you have a license?
2. Who taught you how to drive? Was it easy to learn?
3. Why do teenagers have so many accidents?

Last week, Jennifer celebrated her 16th birthday. She tells her father she wants to learn to drive. He doesn't like the idea at all. But Jennifer insists, and her father finally says she can learn to drive.

Jennifer:	I want to learn to drive.
Father:	Are you kidding? You're only 16.
Jennifer:	That's old enough to get a permit.[1]
Father:	I know, but I won't allow it.
Jennifer:	Why not?
Father:	Who's going to teach you to drive?
Jennifer:	You are, I hope. You're a great driver!
Father:	Don't try to flatter me. I can't teach you to drive.
Jennifer:	Come on, Dad! Don't be mean. What's the problem?
Father:	I have no patience. I'll have a heart attack. I just can't!
Jennifer:	Then, I'll go to a driving school.
Father:	Driving schools are expensive.
Jennifer:	I know, but I have a part-time job. I have the money.
Father:	It'll cost at least $25 an hour.
Jennifer:	I'll learn quickly.
Father:	I still don't like the idea.
Jennifer:	Why not? All my friends are learning to drive.
Father:	Yes, and teenagers have a lot of accidents. Driving is dangerous.
Jennifer:	Don't worry! I'll be a safe driver.
Father:	All right, all right! Go ahead, but drive carefully.
Jennifer:	Thanks, Dad! You're terrific!

---

1. A **permit** allows a learner to drive a car when there is a licensed driver with the learner. In most states, youngsters can get a permit when they reach their 16th or 17th birthday.

COMPREHENSION

Answer these questions in pairs or small groups. Use your own ideas to answer questions with an asterisk.

1. What does Jennifer want to do?
*2. Do you think a person at 16 is old enough to drive? Explain your answer.
3. What does Jennifer say to flatter her father?
4. Why can't her father teach her to drive?
5. What's the problem with going to a driving school?
6. Why doesn't Jennifer's father like the idea of her learning to drive?
*7. Did Jennifer's father make the right decision by finally letting her learn to drive? Explain your answer.

DIALOG REVIEW

Complete the paragraphs with these words.

flatter	**at least**	**kidding**	**go ahead**	**quickly**
dangerous	**permit**	**still**	**expensive**	**enough**

Jennifer tells her father that she wants to learn to drive. He asks her if she is _____ and reminds her that she's only 16. She tells him that's old _____ to get a _____ .

Jennifer wants her father to teach her to drive. She tells him that he's a great driver. He says that she shouldn't try to _____ him, and that he can't teach her to drive because he has no patience.

Jennifer tells her father that she'll go to a driving school. He warns her that driving schools are _____ and that they cost _____ $25 an hour. She says that she has the money and she'll learn _____ , but her father _____ doesn't like the idea.

He tells her that driving is _____ , but she replies that she'll be a safe driver. Her father finally tells her to _____ , but to drive carefully.

SHARING INFORMATION

Discuss these questions in pairs or small groups.

1. Did you learn to drive in your country or in the United States?
2. How old were you when you learned?
3. Do you think it's better to go to a driving school, or to learn from a friend or relative? Explain your answer.
4. Name some things that safe drivers do?
5. Name some things that safe drivers don't do?
6. Do you think you're a safe driver? Explain your answer.
7. Teenagers have to pay more for auto insurance. Why? Do you think that's fair?
8. Why are seat belts so important?
9. In the dialog, Jennifer's father says he has no patience. In general, are you a patient person, or are you like Jennifer's father?
10. Give an example of something that makes you impatient.

DICTATION

1. *Listen while the teacher reads the dialog without stopping. <u>Don't write anything</u>.*

2. *The teacher will read the dialog a second time, pausing after the missing lines. <u>Write in the missing lines</u>.*

3. *The teacher will read the dialog a third time. <u>Check your work</u>.*

Jennifer:	I want to learn to drive.
Father:	_____
Jennifer:	That's old enough to get a permit.
Father:	_____
Jennifer:	Why not?
Father:	_____
Jennifer:	You are, I hope. You're a great driver!
Father:	_____
Jennifer:	Come on, Dad! Don't be mean. What's the problem?
Father:	_____

Our Car Is Falling Apart

1. **borrow** *v.* to receive money from a bank or friend that must be paid back   "Jean borrowed $30 from her cousin and is going to pay her back tomorrow."
2. **brake** *n.* a device that slows or stops a car or other vehicle   "The mechanic is checking the brakes on my car."
3. **fall apart** *idiom*   to be in very bad condition   "Our sofa is falling apart. We have to get a new one."
4. **rest** *n.* what remains   "The first part of the book was interesting, but the rest of it was boring."
5. **service station** *n.* a place that sells gas and repairs cars   "Ben is an auto mechanic. He works at a service station."
6. **tire** *n.* a circular, rubber tube that is put around the wheel of a car   "Your front tires need more air."
7. **waste** *n.* a poor use of   "Talking to Gina is a waste of time. She's not going to help us."

138

PREVIEW QUESTIONS

Discuss these questions before reading the dialog.

1. Do you (or does your family) have a car? If so, what kind?
2. How old is it?
3. Do you have much trouble with it?

Tyrone and Jessica have a car that is nine years old.   Its motor and brakes aren't working very well.   They decide to buy a new car.   They discuss what kind they want and how they can get the money for it.

Tyrone:	We've got a big problem.
Jessica:	What is it?
Tyrone:	Our car is falling apart.
Jessica:	What's wrong with it?
Tyrone:	The motor's not right, and the brakes don't work well.
Jessica:	Can't they repair them at the service station?
Tyrone:	Sure, but it'll cost $900.
Jessica:	That's too much!
Tyrone:	And we'll need new tires pretty[1] soon. Besides, the car is nine years old.
Jessica:	So you're saying it's a waste of money to repair it.
Tyrone:	Exactly. What do you think of buying a Toyota?
Jessica:	Toyotas are good, but I want to buy an American car.
Tyrone:	OK. A friend at work just bought a Saturn,[2] and he loves it.
Jessica:	How much does a Saturn cost?
Tyrone:	About $15,000.
Jessica:	But we don't have that much.
Tyrone:	We've got $8,000 in the bank.
Jessica:	Where are we going to get the rest of the money?
Tyrone:	We've got to borrow it.

---

1. In this line, **pretty** does not mean *beautiful*; it means *quite*. (See *pretty* in the Word Preview section on page 40.)
2. A **Saturn** is a car made in the United States by General Motors.

TRUE OR FALSE

If the sentence is true, write T. *If it's false, write* F.

_____   1. Something is wrong with the motor in Jessica and Tyrone's car.

_____   2. The brakes in their car are OK.

_____   3. The service station can't repair their car.

_____   4. It's a waste of money to repair the car.

_____   5. Tyrone wants to buy a used car.

_____   6. Jessica thinks Toyotas are good, but doesn't want to buy one.

_____   7. Tyrone's friend is happy with his Saturn.

_____   8. Tyrone and Jessica have enough money to buy a new car.

DIALOG REVIEW

Complete the paragraphs with these words.

wrong	besides	borrow	brakes	waste
bought	falling apart	so	rest	pretty

Tyrone and Jessica have got a big problem. Their car is _____. Something is _____ with the motor, and the _____ don't work well.

It'll cost $900 to repair the motor and brakes, and the car will need new tires _____ soon. _____, the car is nine years old. _____ Tyrone thinks it's a _____ of money to repair it.

Tyrone is thinking about buying a Toyota, but Jessica wants an American car. Tyrone says that's OK. His friend at work just _____ a Saturn and loves it.

A Saturn will cost about $15,000, but Tyrone and Jessica have got only $8,000 in the bank. She wants to know where they're going to get the _____ of the money. He says they've got to _____ it.

SHARING INFORMATION

Discuss these questions in pairs or small groups.

1. Are car repairs expensive? If so, why?
2. Do you think that a good auto mechanic who doesn't speak English can get a job in the United States? Explain your answer.
3. Do you do any work on your car? If so, what kind of work do you do?
4. About how much does a small car, like a Toyota Corolla, cost today?
5. About how much does a big car, like a Cadillac, cost?
6. Do you think that American cars are as good as Japanese cars?
7. When it's possible, do you think that people should buy cars and other products made in their own country? Explain your answer.
8. A car dealer is a businessperson who sells cars. Why is it a good idea to go to more than one dealer when you're buying a car?
9. If you were rich, what kind of car would you buy?
10. If you borrow money from a bank to buy a car, who owns the car? You or the bank? Explain your answer.

STORY COMPLETION

An Old Roof and Sidewalk

Mr. and Mrs. Carey live in an old house. They need a new roof, and their sidewalk is also in poor condition. They don't have enough money for the roof or the sidewalk.

Complete the story with these words.

so	**pretty**	**have got to**	**borrow**
wrong	**repair**	**rest**	**soon**

Mr. and Mrs. Carey _____ put a new roof on their house and must also _____ their sidewalk _____ .

They don't have enough money for the roof or the sidewalk, _____ they will have to _____ the money to pay for them.

Fortunately, there is very little _____ with the _____ of the house. It's in _____ good condition.

Canada or Mexico

1. **bay** *n.* an area of the sea partly enclosed by land   "There are many <u>bays</u> along the coast of Cuba."
2. **beach** *n.* an area along the sea or lake covered by sand or small stones   "During the summer, we often go to the <u>beach</u> to swim and lie in the sun."
3. **coin** *n.* a small, round piece of metal used as money   "Pennies, nickels, dimes, and quarters are <u>coins</u> used in the United States."
4. **exciting** *adj.* causing strong feelings and interest   "Our basketball team won the game by one point. It was <u>exciting</u>."
5. **freeze** *v.* to be very cold   "This room is cold. I'm <u>freezing</u>."
6. **give up** *v.* to stop trying   "I'm failing algebra, but I think I can pass if I study hard. I'm not <u>giving up</u>."
7. **head** (often **heads**) *n.* the side of a coin that shows the head of a famous person   "George Washington is on the <u>head</u> of a quarter."
8. **head** *v.* to go in a certain direction   "The bus is <u>heading</u> to Chicago."
9. **selfish** *adj.* caring too much about oneself and not enough about others   "Adam only thinks about what he wants and needs. He's very <u>selfish</u>."
10. **tail** (often **tails**) *n.* the side of a coin that does not have the head of a famous person   "Abraham Lincoln is on the head of a penny, and the Lincoln Memorial is on the <u>tail</u>."
11. **toss** *v.* to throw   "<u>Toss</u> the ball to me."

142

PREVIEW QUESTIONS

Discuss these questions before reading the dialog.

1. Where is Canada located? Were you ever there? What do you know about its history? about its climate?
2. Where is Mexico located? Were you ever there? What do you know about its history? about its climate?
3. What languages are spoken in Canada? in Mexico?

Dan and Kelly are married and live in New York City. Dan wants to go to Canada for their vacation, and Kelly wants to go to Mexico. They argue and then decide to toss a coin to settle their argument.

Dan:	I want to go to Canada this summer.
Kelly:	I want to go to Mexico.
Dan:	But Mexico is too hot.
Kelly:	And Canada is too cold. I'll freeze!
Dan:	Not in the summer, you won't.
Kelly:	But Mexico is beautiful and exciting.
Dan:	So is Canada. What's more exciting and beautiful than Niagara Falls?
Kelly:	The beaches and bay of Acapulco.
Dan:	I also want to see Montreal and practice my French.
Kelly:	And I want to see Mexico City and practice my Spanish.
Dan:	Aren't you being a little selfish?
Kelly:	No more than you.
Dan:	Well, Canada is closer. We can drive there in six hours.
Kelly:	And we can fly to Mexico in four.
Dan:	Let's stop arguing. I have an idea.
Kelly:	It better[1] be good.
Dan:	We can toss a coin to decide.
Kelly:	OK. Heads, I win.[2]
Dan:	It's tails. You lose. It looks like we're heading to Canada.
Kelly:	And next summer to Mexico.
Dan:	You never give up, do you?
Kelly:	No, why should I?

1. **Better** in this line is short for *had better*. "It better be good." = "It *had better* be good."
2. Dan throws a coin in the air to decide their argument. Kelly bets that the **head** of the coin will face up. But it faces down, so she loses.

COMPREHENSION

Answer these questions in pairs or small groups. Use your own ideas to answer questions with an asterisk.

1. What does Dan say is the problem with Mexico?
2. What does Kelly say is the problem with Canada?
3. What does Dan want to practice? And Kelly?
*4. Do you think they are both being selfish? Explain your answer.
5. How does Dan want to decide where they're going?
*6. What do you think of his idea?
7. Who wins the toss of the coin?

DIALOG REVIEW

Complete the paragraphs with these words.

bay	heading	selfish	gives up	arguing
toss	freeze	better	tails	exciting

Dan wants to go to Canada, but his wife, Kelly, wants to go to Mexico. He says that Mexico is too hot. She replies that Canada is too cold, and she'll

_____ .

Dan asks what's more _____ and beautiful than Niagara Falls. Kelly replies the beaches and _____ of Acapulco.

Dan thinks that Kelly is being a little _____ , and she thinks he is too. He suggests that they stop _____ . He has an idea. Kelly says that it _____ be good.

Dan says that they can _____ a coin to decide. That's OK with Kelly. If it's heads, she wins. But it's _____ , and she loses. So they're _____ to Canada.

But she says that next year they're going to Mexico. She never

_____ .

SHARING INFORMATION

Discuss these questions in pairs or small groups.

1. Do you think most married couples argue a lot? If so, why?
2. How often do you argue? (a) frequently (b) sometimes (c) rarely (d) never
3. Who do you argue with?
4. What do you argue about?
5. How long is your vacation?
6. Do you usually go somewhere on your vacation? If so, where?
7. Do you have any coins from your country? If so, bring some to school to show to the class.
8. Many people collect coins or stamps or baseball cards. Do you collect anything? If so, what?
9. Did you ever visit Niagara Falls, Montreal, Acapulco, or Mexico City? If so, tell us about your visit(s).
10. If you could visit Canada or Mexico, which country would you visit? Why?

MATCHING

Match the words in Column A with their definitions or descriptions in Column B. Print the letters on the blank lines.

Column A	Column B
_____ 1. beach	A. to stop trying
_____ 2. brakes	B. we put air in it
_____ 3. rest	C. to go in a certain direction
_____ 4. selfish	D. to be in very bad condition
_____ 5. give up	E. what remains
_____ 6. patience	F. to be very cold
_____ 7. head (verb)	G. the ability to accept calmly what one doesn't like
_____ 8. permit	H. a nice place to go in the summer
_____ 9. fall apart	I. used as money
_____ 10. freeze	J. a paper or card saying you can do something
_____ 11. tire	K. what you use to stop a car
_____ 12. coin	L. never thinking of others

Wild Bill

1. **degree** *n.* a title that a college or university gives to a student who has completed a course of study   "Mary Ellen has a B.A. (Bachelor of Arts) degree in English literature from New York University."
2. **dumb** (informal) *adj.* stupid; not smart   "Keith needs a lawyer, but he won't see one. I think that's dumb."
3. **encourage** *v.* to urge a person to do something: to give hope to someone   "Lisa's parents encouraged her to go to college."   "The victory encouraged our team."
4. **except** (**for**) *prep.* but not; not including   "Everyone went swimming except Mike."
5. **interest** *n.* a desire to know, learn, or see something   "Music is one of Eddie's many interests." *Interest* is also used as a verb.   "Baseball doesn't interest me."
6. **joy** *n.* great happiness   "Seeing our grandchildren brings us a lot of joy."
7. **live up to** *idiom* to live or act as others expect   "Everyone thinks that Henry is very kind, and he tries to live up to what people think."
8. **motivate** *v.* to give a person a reason to do something; to cause a person to act   "Money motivates people to work hard."
9. **neither** *adj.* not one or the other of two   "Neither band played well."
10. **not . . . at all** *idiom*   not . . . in any way   "Brenda did not help us at all."
11. **on duty** *idiom*   working at one's job at this time (said especially of soldiers, police officers, and nurses)   "There's always a soldier on duty at the gate of the camp."
12. **pride** *n.* a feeling of satisfaction in what one does or has   "Sal is a good carpenter, and he takes pride in his work."
13. **quit** *v.* to stop doing something; to leave school or a job   "Lauren is going to quit her job because her pay is very low."
14. **race** *v.* to try to run or drive faster than another   "I'll race you to the house."
15. **sports car** *n.* a two-passenger car with extra power and speed   "Let me take you for a ride in my sports car. You'll love it!"
16. **sympathetic** *adj.* feeling sympathy (*Sympathy* is the act of sharing the feelings and problems of another.)   "I like to discuss my problems with my friend Marge. She's sympathetic."
17. **threaten** *v.* to warn that one may punish   "The teacher threatened to fail me."
18. **wild** *adj.* without control   "Stan and Dianne's kids are pretty wild."

PREVIEW QUESTIONS

Discuss these questions before reading the dialog.

1. How is a sports car different from an ordinary car? Are sports cars more expensive?
2. What makes some teachers and classes interesting and others boring?
3. Do you think auto mechanics have a good job? Explain your answer. Do they make good money?

Everyone calls him "Wild Bill," and he lives up to his name. Three things are important to Bill—cars, money, and a girl named Megan. Bill is 24, and last month he bought a new sports car. The car cost $25,000, and it's his pride and joy.

When Bill drives on a highway, he usually goes 70 to 80 miles an hour. Bill and his friend Charley also like to race on Route 3 at one or two in the morning. There is almost no traffic at that hour, and only a few police cars are on duty.

Except for his science class, school didn't interest Bill at all. He thought his classes were boring, and his lack of interest annoyed his teachers. The sympathetic ones tried to understand and encourage Bill. The strict ones threatened him. But neither was able to motivate him. "I never did any homework, and I rarely paid attention in class, so I can't blame the teachers for getting angry," he says. Bill quit school at 16.

Bill isn't dumb or lazy, however. He works hard and is smart. He knows everything there is to know about cars, and he's very good at fixing them. After he quit school, he got a job as a mechanic at an auto repair shop. He's still working there, and he's making more money than many people with college degrees.

TRUE OR FALSE

If the sentence is true, write T. *If it's false, write* F.

_____   1. Bill is proud of his new sports car.

_____   2. He is careful to obey traffic laws.

_____   3. Charley and Bill like to race when there is little traffic.

_____   4. Bill was interested in his science class.

_____   5. The strict teachers were able to get him to do his homework.

_____   6. Bill couldn't get a job when he quit school.

_____   7. He is more successful at work than he was in school.

_____   8. Bill's salary is low.

STORY COMPLETION

Our Basketball Coach

Mr. Florio is our high-school basketball coach, and he loves the game. He has his team practice long hours, and he gets along well with his players.

Complete the story with these words.

motivating	quit	annoys	interests
blame	except	pride	at all

Mr. Florio is our high-school basketball coach, and his team practices every day of the week _____ Sunday.   Nothing _____ him more than basketball.

Coach Florio is very good at _____ his players, and he takes great _____ in them.   His players also like him, and it's rare for one of them to _____ the team.

Coach Florio doesn't like it _____ when his team loses, but he doesn't _____ the players if they did their best. Of course, it really _____ him if the team loses because the players didn't try hard enough.

SHARING INFORMATION

Discuss these questions in pairs or small groups. Space is provided to write your answers if you wish.

1. What are some of the differences between schools in the United States and in your country?

   _____

   _____

2. What can teachers do to motivate students to do their best?

   _____

   _____

3. What can parents do?

   _____

   _____

4. Do you think it was OK for Bill to quit school, or do you think he should have finished high school before going to work as a mechanic? Explain your answer.

   _____

   _____

5. What kind of job would you like to have? What do you have to do to get it?

   _____

   _____

6. Give some examples of people who have jobs that pay well but don't require a high-school education (for example, a carpenter).

   _____

   _____

7. Give some examples of people who have jobs that require a high-school but not a college education. Include jobs that require training (for example, a beautician).

   _____

   _____

8. Give some examples of people who have jobs that require a college education. Include jobs that require more than a college education (for example, a lawyer).

   _____

   _____

Lucky to be Alive

WORD PREVIEW

1. **adore** *v.* to love and honor deeply "Ron <u>adores</u> his wife."
2. **bleed** *v.* to lose blood "My nose is <u>bleeding</u>."
3. **damage** *n.* a loss of value "The fire did a lot of <u>damage</u> to our house."
4. **date** *v.* to go on a date (A *date* is a meeting of an unmarried couple to go out to dinner, a movie, a dance, etc.) "Wayne and Amy are <u>dating</u>."
5. **disco** *n.* a nightclub where people, especially young people, go to dance to modern music "Every Saturday night Tanya and I go to a <u>disco</u> to dance and listen to the music."
6. **in time** *idiom* early enough; soon enough "Ralph came <u>in time</u> to see the beginning of the show."
7. **midnight** *n.* twelve o'clock at night "The party ended around <u>midnight</u>."
8. **obviously** *adv.* clearly "Regina's apartment has a lot of books. She <u>obviously</u> likes to read."
9. **slam** *v.* to throw or hit with great force "I was so angry that I <u>slammed</u> my book on the desk."
10. **slow down** *v.* to go slower "You better <u>slow down</u>—you're speeding again."
11. **stitch** *n.* the thread sewn in a cut to close it and stop the bleeding "The cut was bad and needed 12 <u>stitches</u>."
12. **suddenly** *adv.* happening quickly and without warning "<u>Suddenly</u>, it started to rain."
13. **wear** *v.* to have on one's body "Joan <u>wears</u> eyeglasses."

PREVIEW QUESTIONS

Discuss these questions before reading the dialog.

1. Why is it dangerous to drink before you drive?
2. Why is it dangerous to drive fast when it's raining?
3. Were you ever in an auto accident? If so, describe what happened.

Megan is Bill's girlfriend, and they have been dating for a year. He adores her, and she's crazy about him. Last Saturday, Bill took her to the movies. After the movies, they stopped at a disco. Both of them like to dance, and Megan is an excellent dancer. Bill's pretty good too, but not as good as Megan. They each had a couple of drinks and something to eat, and left the disco at midnight.

It began to rain hard as they started to drive home. Bill was speeding down Route 17 at 75 miles an hour. Suddenly, the car in front of him slowed down. Bill slammed on his brakes, but he couldn't stop in time. He hit the car in front of him. They had to rush Bill to the hospital, but fortunately, no one else was hurt.

Bill's car has an air bag, but he wasn't wearing his seat belt. He broke his arm and cut his forehead. He needed 12 stitches to stop the bleeding, and he's still in the hospital. He's lucky to be alive.

It'll cost $5,000 to repair Bill's car. His insurance company also has to pay for the damage to the other car. The accident was obviously his fault. "I'll never drive so fast again," Wild Bill says. His friends hope that's true, but they don't really believe it.

COMPREHENSION

Answer these questions in pairs or small groups. Use your own ideas to answer questions with an asterisk.

1. How long have Bill and Megan been dating?
2. Where did they go after the movies?
*3. Why was it a good idea for Bill to eat something at the disco?
4. How fast was Bill driving?
5. What did he do when the car in front of him slowed down?
6. Was Megan hurt in the accident? How badly was Bill hurt?
7. Why does Bill's insurance company have to pay for the damage to the other car?
*8. What is going to happen to the cost of Bill's car insurance?

STORY COMPLETION

She Hit a Tree

Melissa was riding her bike down a big hill. Her bike went off the road and hit a tree. Her face and hands were cut, and she hurt her leg. An ambulance took her to the hospital.

Complete the story with these words.

stitches	brakes	wearing	slow down
slammed	rushed	bleeding	broke

Melissa was riding her bike down a big hill. She decided to _____, but when she tried to put on her _____, they didn't work.

Melissa went off the road and _____ into a tree. Fortunately, she was _____ a helmet, but she cut her face and hands and _____ her leg. An ambulance _____ to the scene of the accident and took Melissa to the hospital.

She needed 20 _____ to stop the _____.

SHARING INFORMATION

Discuss these questions in pairs or small groups. Space is provided to write your answers if you wish.

1. Do you prefer to go to the movies or to watch them at home on a VCR? Explain your answer.

   _____

   _____

2. Bill had a couple of drinks at the disco. Do you think this was one of the causes of his accident? Explain your answer.

   _____

   _____

3. The United States had a national speed limit of 55 miles per hour, but Congress changed that. Today states can allow a higher limit and most do. Do you think the change was a good idea? Explain your answer.

   _____

   _____

4. Do you think Bill will drive more slowly in the future because of his accident? Explain your answer.

   _____

   _____

5. If a driver has an accident, what information does he or she have to give to the other driver?

   _____

   _____

6. Why should you call the police if you have an accident?

   _____

   _____

7. All new cars must have air bags. Does that mean that seat belts are no longer important? Explain your answer.

   _____

   _____

8. Does your state have a law that all drivers must use their seat belts? Do you always use yours?

   _____

   _____

SYNONYMS

Synonyms are words that have the same or a similar meaning. In the blank spaces, write a synonym for the underlined word or words.

except	obviously	lucky	terrific	toss
at least	suddenly	pretty	repair	have got to

1.   The children like to <u>throw</u> rocks into the lake. _____
2.   It's <u>quite</u> hot today. _____
3.   Everyone <u>but</u> Roger passed the exam. _____
4.   I <u>must</u> paint the kitchen. _____
5.   Mrs. Chang died <u>without warning</u>. _____
6.   Bogdan is a <u>great</u> soccer player. _____
7.   The trip will take <u>a minimum of</u> three hours. _____
8.   Ann has good health, a great job, and lots of friends. She's very <u>fortunate</u>. _____
9.   The plumber is going to <u>fix</u> the pipe. _____
10. Dr. Jordan has a big house and lots of money. <u>Clearly</u>, he's rich. _____

ANTONYMS

Antonyms are words that have opposite meanings. In the blank spaces, write an antonym for each word.

alive	dumb	quit	in front of	pride
mean	kid	flatter	waste	expensive

1.   smart _____
2.   cheap _____
3.   criticize _____
4.   kind _____
5.   behind _____
6.   be serious _____
7.   shame _____
8.   begin _____
9.   dead _____
10. use well _____

8

WOMEN
AND
DECISIONS

A Siren and Flashing Lights

WORD PREVIEW

1. **cop** (very informal) *n.* a policeman or policewoman "There were two <u>cops</u> standing outside the bank."
2. **flash** (said of a light) *v.* to go on and off quickly "The lights on the ambulance are <u>flashing</u>."
3. **officer** (a term of respect) *n.* a policeman or policewoman "Excuse me, <u>Officer</u>. Is it OK to park here?"
4. **pull over** *v.* to drive a car or truck to the side of the road "The truck <u>pulled over</u> and parked."
5. **siren** *n.* a device on a police car, ambulance, or fire engine that makes a loud noise to warn other drivers "When I heard the <u>siren</u>, I pulled over and let the fire engine pass."
6. **ticket** *n.* a written notice to pay money or to appear in court for not obeying a traffic law "The police officer gave me a <u>ticket</u> for driving too fast."
7. **used to** *idiom* done in the past but not done now; true in the past but not true now "Ric <u>used to</u> play basketball." "Mr. Patel <u>used to</u> live in India." "Texas <u>used to</u> be part of Mexico."

PREVIEW QUESTIONS

Discuss these questions before reading the dialog.

1. What is the speed limit in your state?
2. Is it possible to speed a lot and still be a good driver? Explain your answer.
3. If a police officer stops someone for speeding, does the person usually get a ticket?

A year after their accident, Bill and Megan got married. Bill never speeds anymore. Now it's Megan who drives too fast. Megan and Bill are going to a movie. It starts in a few minutes, and Megan is driving.

Bill:	Hey, Megan, you're driving too fast!
Megan:	Well, we're in a hurry. The movie starts in a few minutes.
Bill:	I know, but you're going 70![1]
Megan:	Relax! Nothing is going to happen. I'm a good driver.
Bill:	Good drivers don't speed the way you do.
Megan:	Look who's talking! You used to speed all the time.
Bill:	Yes, but I'm warning you—some day a cop is going to stop you.
Megan:	Maybe. But I won't get a ticket.
Bill:	Why not?
Megan:	I'll tell him my aunt is dying, and I'm rushing to the hospital to see her.
Bill:	He'll never believe you.
Megan:	Maybe he will. You never know.
Bill:	Is that a siren I hear?
Megan:	Yes. It must be an ambulance or a fire engine.
Bill:	Sorry, dear. It's[2] a police car, and its lights are flashing.
Megan:	Oh, no! Is he stopping us?
Bill:	I think so. You better slow down and pull over.
Megan:	OK. But let me do the talking.
Bill:	I will. It's your problem.
Megan:	I just hope the officer is nice.

---

1. **Going 70** means *going 70 miles per hour.* "How fast are you going?" "I'm going 60."
2. Notice the difference between **it's** = *it is* and the possessive adjective **its**. The possessive adjective *its* never has an apostrophe.

COMPREHENSION

Answer these questions in pairs or small groups. Use your own ideas to answer questions with an asterisk.

1. How fast is Megan driving?
2. Why is she driving so fast?
*3. Do you think she's foolish to drive so fast to get to a movie on time? Explain your answer.
4. What is Megan going to tell the police officer if she gets stopped?
5. What does Bill tell her she better do?
*6. Why do you think that she wants to do the talking?
7. What does she hope?

DIALOG REVIEW

Complete the paragraphs with these words.

used to	flashing	ticket	in a hurry	better
dying	relax	pull over	believe	cop

Megan and Bill are going to a movie that starts in a few minutes. They're _____ , and Megan is going 70. Bill tells her that she's going too fast. She tells him to _____ , that nothing is going to happen. She also reminds him that he _____ speed all the time.

Bill warns Megan that some day a _____ is going to stop her. She knows that may happen, but she says she won't get a _____ . Bill asks her why not. She says she'll tell the officer that her aunt is _____ and that she's rushing to the hospital to see her. Bill says the officer will never _____ her.

Bill hears a siren. Megan thinks it's an ambulance or a fire engine. He tells her it's a police car and that its lights are _____ . He also tells her that she _____ slow down and _____ . She hopes the officer is nice.

SHARING INFORMATION

Discuss these questions in pairs or small groups.

1. Name something that you used to do, but that you don't do anymore.
2. Do you like to drive fast? How often do you go over the speed limit?
   (a) never (b) sometimes (c) frequently
3. Did you ever get stopped for speeding? Did you get a ticket?
4. Did you ever get a parking ticket? Do you get a lot of them?
5. About how much are most speeding tickets? most parking tickets?
6. Are you uncomfortable in a car in which the driver is going very fast?
7. Do some people drive too slowly? Why is this dangerous?
8. Are police officers and traffic laws stricter in your country or in the United States?
9. Is there a difference in the way people drive in your country and in the United States? If so, what's the difference?
10. Do you think most police officers are nice? Explain your answer.

DICTATION

1. Listen while the teacher reads the dialog without stopping. <u>Don't write anything</u>.

2. The teacher will read the dialog a second time, pausing after the missing lines. <u>Write in the missing lines</u>.

3. The teacher will read the dialog a third time. <u>Check your work</u>.

Bill: Hey, Megan, you're driving too fast!

Megan: _____

Bill: I know, but you're going 70!

Megan: _____

Bill: Good drivers don't speed the way you do.

Megan: _____

Bill: Yes, but I'm warning you—some day a cop is going to stop you.

Megan: _____

Bill: Why not?

Megan: _____

Are You Deaf, Lady?

WORD PREVIEW

1. **accurate** *adj.* exact; with no errors "The accident report is <u>accurate</u>."
2. **by the way** *idiom* to introduce a new but related idea; also "I'm going to the bank to cash my check. Oh, <u>by the way</u>, don't you still owe me $20?"
3. **deaf** *adj.* not able to hear "Cindy can't hear you. She's <u>deaf</u>."
4. **extremely** *adv.* very "I'm <u>extremely</u> tired. I better lie down."
5. **license** *n.* a card issued by the state, giving a person permission to drive "You can't drive without a <u>license</u>."
6. **loud** *adj.* producing a strong sound "Turn down the TV—it's too <u>loud</u>."
7. **radar** *n.* a device that uses radio waves to show how fast a car is going "You should slow down. The police on this highway use <u>radar</u>."
8. **realize** *v.* to know "I didn't <u>realize</u> that Erica was a judge."
9. **registration** *n.* a card issued by the state, describing a car and giving the name and address of its owner "Never leave your <u>registration</u> in your car. Keep it in your wallet."
10. **stroke** *n.* sudden damage to the brain caused by the blocking or breaking of a blood vessel leading to the brain "Victor can't speak clearly. He had a <u>stroke</u>."
11. **traffic light** *n.* a set of red, yellow, and green lights that control traffic on busy streets and highways "We need a <u>traffic light</u> at this corner—there have been too many accidents here."

PREVIEW QUESTIONS

Discuss these questions before reading the dialog.

1. Did a police officer ever stop a car you were in? Why did the officer stop the car?
2. Did the officer ask for the driver's license and registration?
3. Describe the way the officer acted. Was the officer polite? unpleasant? angry?

Jim Kropke is a police officer, and he stops Megan for speeding. She's very polite and calls him "officer" as much as possible. She tells him that they're rushing to the hospital to visit her aunt who is very sick. Jim asks for her license and registration. Do you think he'll give her a ticket?

Jim:	What took[1] you so long to stop?
Megan:	For a while, I didn't hear the siren, Officer.
Jim:	That's an extremely loud siren. Are you deaf, lady?
Megan:	My hearing is fine. What's the problem, Officer?
Jim:	You were speeding.
Megan:	Me? Speeding?[2] Are you sure?
Jim:	Absolutely. Our radar is very accurate.
Megan:	How fast was I going?
Jim:	Seventy.
Megan:	I didn't realize that. We're rushing to the hospital. My aunt is very sick.
Jim:	I don't care who's sick.
Megan:	But it's an emergency! She had a stroke! She may die!
Jim:	Let's see your license and registration.
Megan:	Of course, Officer. They're in my handbag. Here you are.
Jim:	Megan Keller. Ford. Four door, blue. Taurus.[3] OK, Mrs. Keller.
Megan:	By the way, Officer, where do we turn to get to the hospital?
Jim:	Make a right turn at the next traffic light.
Megan:	You're not going to give me a ticket, are you?
Jim:	Not this time, lady, but slow down.
Megan:	All right. Thank you, Officer. Have a nice day!

1. **Took** is the past tense of *take*. *Take* is often used to indicate the amount of time needed to do something. "It takes ten minutes to walk to the park." "Why does it take so long to learn a new language?"
2. **Me? Speeding?** Megan raises her voice at the end of these words to make them questions.
3. **Megan Keller. Ford. Four door, blue. Taurus.** Jim is reading these words from Megan's registration. The Taurus is Ford's most popular car.

TRUE OR FALSE

If the sentence is true, write T. If it's false, write F.

_____ 1. Jim thinks Megan took too long to stop.

_____ 2. He asks her about her ability to hear.

_____ 3. She says she can't hear well.

_____ 4. Jim doesn't trust his radar.

_____ 5. Megan tells him that her aunt had a heart attack.

_____ 6. Megan doesn't want to show him her license and registration.

_____ 7. Jim tells her how to get to the hospital.

_____ 8. He doesn't give Megan a ticket, but warns her to slow down.

DIALOG REVIEW

Complete the paragraphs with these words.

loud	stroke	absolutely	while	registration
accurate	took	turn	realize	deaf

Jim, a police officer, asks Megan why it _____ her so long to stop. She replies that for a _____ she didn't hear the siren. Jim tells her that the siren is extremely _____ and asks her if she's _____ . She replies that her hearing is fine.

Megan asks Jim what the problem is. He tells her that she was speeding, and that he's _____ sure of this because his radar is very _____ .

Megan asks how fast she was going. Jim tells her she was going 70. She says she didn't _____ that, and she tells him that she's rushing to the hospital to visit her aunt who had a _____ and may die.

Jim asks for Megan's license and _____ . He checks them and says they're OK. Megan asks him where to _____ to get to the hospital. He tells her and warns her to slow down, but doesn't give her a ticket.

SHARING INFORMATION

Discuss these questions in pairs or small groups.

1. Do the police in your state frequently use radar to catch drivers who are speeding?
2. Do the police in your country frequently use radar to catch speeders?
3. Must drivers always have their license and registration with them?
4. Do they need to have anything else? If so, what?
5. Why do police officers ask for a driver's license and registration when they stop a car?
6. Megan was very polite to Jim. Do you think that helped her not to get a ticket? Explain your answer.
7. Do you think it was wrong for her to tell Jim a lie? Explain your answer.
8. Do you think most police officers would have given Megan a ticket? Explain your answer.
9. If you were a police officer, would you have given her a ticket?
10. Do you think she will continue to speed in the future? Explain your answer.

STORY COMPLETION

My Grandmother

My grandmother is 85 years old. Last month, they had to take her to the hospital. She's much better now, but it's still difficult for her to speak.

Complete the story with these words.

officer	loud	realized	deaf
extremely	while	took	stroke

My grandmother is 85, and last month she had a _____ .

She was living alone, and it was a _____ before a neighbor

_____ she needed help and called 911.

A police _____ came to the house at once and called an

ambulance. It _____ the ambulance three minutes to arrive.

My grandmother is much better now, but it's still _____

difficult for her to talk. In addition, she's almost _____ , and

we have to speak to her in a _____ voice.

The Old Approach

POLICE

WORD PREVIEW

1. **approach** *n.* a way of doing something "The students aren't learning much. The teacher should try a different <u>approach</u>."
2. **be in favor of** *idiom* to support or believe in something "Most people <u>are in favor of</u> lower taxes."
3. **close call** *idiom* something bad almost happens "That was a <u>close call</u>! Our plane almost crashed into a mountain."
4. **complicated** *adj.* difficult to understand or do "I can't do these math problems. They're too <u>complicated</u>."
5. **credit** *n.* approval; praise "Gary isn't a very good basketball player, but you have to give him <u>credit</u> for trying."
6. **deal with** *v.* to work with; to handle "It isn't easy to <u>deal with</u> teenagers."
7. **deserve** *v.* should receive "Sandra works hard and is an excellent secretary. She <u>deserves</u> more money."
8. **parrot** *n.* a tropical bird famous for repeating what it hears "Our <u>parrot</u> never stops talking."
9. **polite** *adj.* having good manners; thoughtful of others "Mario always says 'thank you' and 'please.' He's a <u>polite</u> little boy."
10. **proud (of)** *adj.* to be very satisfied or pleased with "I'm <u>proud of</u> my family."
11. **women's lib** (short for **women's liberation**) *n.* a movement that seeks more freedom and equal opportunities for women (*Liberation* is the act of freeing or the condition of being free.) "It's difficult for Glenn to accept <u>women's liberation</u>. He's old-fashioned."

PREVIEW QUESTIONS

Discuss these questions before reading the dialog.

1. If you were stopped by a police officer, would you be very polite? Explain your answer.
2. In the last dialog (page 161), do you think Megan was lucky not to get a ticket when the police officer stopped her for speeding? Explain your answer.
3. What does the expression *women's liberation* mean to you?

Megan and Bill are discussing how she talked to Jim, the police officer. Bill thinks she was lucky. She agrees, but thinks she deserves some credit for her acting. She also says she knows how to deal with men. Bill wants to know what she means.

Bill:	That was a close call, Megan! You were lucky you didn't get a ticket.
Megan:	That's right, but I also deserve some credit.
Bill:	For what? For lying?
Megan:	No, I'm not proud of that.
Bill:	What are you proud of?
Megan:	My acting.
Bill:	It was good. You were so polite I almost laughed!
Megan:	You have to be polite when you're wrong.
Bill:	You sounded like a parrot. "What's the problem, Officer? Of course, Officer. By the way, Officer. Thank you, Officer."
Megan:	I know how to deal with men.
Bill:	What do you mean?
Megan:	You let a man think he's the boss.
Bill:	And you get what you want.
Megan:	Exactly.
Bill:	Isn't[1] that old-fashioned?
Megan:	Yes, and it works every time.
Bill:	But you're modern and in favor of women's lib.
Megan:	Of course! But sometimes I still use the old approach.
Bill:	Women are complicated.
Megan:	No. Just smart. We have to be!

---

1. **Isn't** introduces a negative question. Negative questions expect the answer *yes*. "<u>Isn't</u> the baby cute?"

COMPREHENSION

Answer these questions in pairs or small groups. Use your own ideas to answer questions with an asterisk.

1. Why was Megan lucky?
2. What is she proud of?
3. Why did Bill almost laugh?
4. How does Megan deal with men?
*5. What do you think of her way of dealing with men? Do you think it works?
6. Megan is modern, but what does she sometimes use?
*7. Why do you think she says women have to be smart?

DIALOG REVIEW

Complete the paragraphs with these words.

old-fashioned	approach	proud	means	deserves
complicated	polite	deal with	in favor of	sounded

Bill thinks Megan was lucky not to get a ticket. She agrees, but says that she _____ some credit.

Megan says she isn't _____ of lying, but of her acting. She was so _____ to the police officer that Bill almost laughed, and she repeated the word *officer* so much that she _____ like a parrot.

Megan says she knows how to _____ men. Bill wants to know what she _____ by that. She explains that you let a man think that he's the boss and you get what you want. Bill asks her if that isn't _____. She says it is, and that it works all the time.

Although Megan is modern and _____ women's lib, sometimes she still uses the old _____.

Bill says that women are _____, but Megan replies that women are just smart. They have to be.

SHARING INFORMATION

Discuss these questions in pairs or small groups.

1. How important is it to be polite? Explain your answer.
2. Give some examples of polite words and actions.
3. Do you think you're modern or old-fashioned? or both? Explain your answer.
4. Megan did a good job of acting. Why is acting important to the lawyer in the courtroom and the teacher in the classroom?
5. Do women in the United States have as many opportunities for good jobs as men?
6. Do women in your country have as many?
7. Name some jobs and professions that more women are entering today than 20 years ago.
8. Do women in the United States have more freedom than women in your country? Explain your answer.
9. The Spanish words *macho* and *machismo* have become part of the English language. What is machismo? How do you feel about machismo?
10. Is machismo stronger in your country or in the United States?

MATCHING

Match the words in Column A with their definitions or descriptions in Column B. Print the letters on the blank lines.

Column A   **Column B**

_____ 1. stroke   A. you need one to drive

_____ 2. deaf   B. very satisfied with

_____ 3. close call   C. done in the past, but not done now

_____ 4. proud of   D. exact

_____ 5. siren   E. what you get for speeding

_____ 6. accurate   F. not able to hear

_____ 7. license   G. praise

_____ 8. flash   H. something bad almost happens

_____ 9. credit   I. the police use this to check speed

_____ 10. used to   J. it damages the brain

_____ 11. radar   K. to go on and off quickly

_____ 12. ticket   L. it makes a loud noise

The Extra Money Would Help

1. **cheerful** *adj.* happy "Jackie smiles a lot and is always <u>cheerful</u>."
2. **curious** *adj.* having a strong desire to know "We want the students to be <u>curious</u>."
3. **efficient** *adj.* working well and without wasting time or energy "Our new boss is <u>efficient</u>. She knows how to get things done."
4. **engineering** *n.* the science and profession of planning and building roads, bridges, machines, etc. "Yuri wants to study <u>engineering</u> in college."
5. **even** *adv.* more than expected; surprisingly (*Even* gives emphasis to the words that follow it.) "Paula goes to work <u>even</u> when she doesn't feel well."
6. **former** *adj.* was in the past; earlier "I want you to meet a <u>former</u> student of mine. He's a teacher now."
7. **get into** *v.* to put oneself into something, often bad "Hector <u>got into</u> a fight after school."
8. **injure** *v.* to hurt; to damage "Three people were <u>injured</u> in the accident."
9. **off duty** *idiom* not working at one's job at this time (said especially of soldiers, police officers, and nurses) "The soldiers like to play cards when they're <u>off duty</u>."
10. **paperwork** *n.* the work of writing and filing reports, letters, and records "The secretary does most of the boss's <u>paperwork</u>."
11. **personnel** *n.* all the people who work for a company or an organization "A company is only as good as its <u>personnel</u>."
12. **position** *n.* job "Carl has a very good <u>position</u> and makes a lot of money."
13. **reason** *n.* the motive or cause of an action "There are several <u>reasons</u> why Ashley wants to be a doctor."

168

PREVIEW QUESTIONS

Discuss these questions before reading the story.

1. Young children are very curious. Why is this good? What problems can it cause?
2. Police work is dangerous. Do you think that the wives and husbands of police officers ever stop worrying about them? Explain your answer.
3. The mother of two children—a three-year-old girl and a six-year-old boy—has a good job offer. The family can live without the additional money, but it would help. Do you think she should take the job or stay home and take care of the children? Explain your answer.

   Jim and Betty are married and have two children, Brian and Michelle. Brian is six years old and Michelle is three. Brian is in the first grade. He loves school and can read quite well for a first-grade student. Michelle is very curious. She's always asking questions and gets into everything.

Jim is a police officer—he's the one who stopped Megan for speeding. He earns $48,000 a year. His job is dangerous, but he likes it. Betty worries a lot about him. She's afraid that some day he will be injured or killed. He carries a gun even when he's off duty.

Betty stays home and takes care of Michelle and Brian. She knows how important this is, and it certainly keeps her busy. However, there are times when she thinks about returning to her old job. She used to work in the personnel department of a large engineering company. She gets along well with all kinds of people and is always cheerful. She's also very efficient and good at handling paperwork.

Two days ago, Betty's former boss called and offered her the position of personnel director. She doesn't have to take the job. The family can live on Jim's salary. However, prices keep going up, and the extra money would help a lot. Betty doesn't know what to do. She sees good reasons to take the job and good reasons to stay home.

TRUE OR FALSE

If the sentence is true, write T. *If it's false, write* F.

_____ 1. Brian is a good reader, but he doesn't like school.

_____ 2. Michelle asks a lot of questions and likes to explore things.

_____ 3. Although Jim's job is dangerous, he likes it.

_____ 4. Sometimes Betty thinks about going back to her old job.

_____ 5. She used to work as an engineer.

_____ 6. She has an opportunity to go back to work.

_____ 7. Jim's salary isn't big enough to support his family.

_____ 8. Betty feels certain she should go back to work.

STORY COMPLETION

Our History Teacher

Our history teacher's name is Mr. Kaminski. He's always happy, and most of the students like him. He loves to read about history, and he loved to play basketball, but he hurt his back and can't play anymore.

paperwork	**used to**	**cheerful**	**efficient**
injured	**gets along**	**quite**	**curious**

Our history teacher's name is Mr. Kaminski, and I like him a lot. He's always _____ and _____ well with the other teachers and most of the students.

Mr. Kaminski is very_____ and loves to read, especially about history. He also likes to visit historic places. However, he doesn't like _____ and isn't very _____, so it takes him a long time to correct our tests.

Mr. Kaminski _____ play a lot of basketball, and he was _____ good, but he _____ his back and can't play anymore.

SHARING INFORMATION

Discuss these questions in pairs or small groups. Space is provided to write your answers if you wish.

1. Why do you think Jim carries a gun even when he's off duty?

    _____

    _____

2. Police work is very dangerous. How would you feel if your child (or brother or sister) decided to become a police officer?

    _____

    _____

3. Do you think that $48,000 a year is enough for a family of four to live on? Explain your answer.

    _____

    _____

4. What does a personnel director do? Do you think it's an interesting job?

    _____

    _____

5. (question for women) If you had no young children and your family didn't need the money, would you prefer to stay home or to go out to work? Explain your answer.

    _____

    _____

6. (question for men) If you had no young children and your family didn't need the money, would you prefer that your wife stay home or go out to work? Explain your answer.

    _____

    _____

7. In your country, do most married women who don't have young children to care for have a job outside the home?

    _____

    _____

8. In general, are married women who work more independent of their husbands? Explain your answer.

    _____

    _____

A Tough Decision

VICE-PRESIDENT

WORD PREVIEW

1. **advice** *n.* an opinion one gives to another to help that person with a problem "Fran wants to buy a computer and needs some advice."

2. **away** *adv.* at a distance "Milt lives a block away from the ocean."

3. **concerned (about)** *adj.* worried (about); anxious "We're having a picnic tomorrow, and I'm concerned about the weather."

4. **decision** *n.* the act or result of choosing; choice "Greg and Sonia made a decision to sell their house and move to Arizona."

5. **face** *v.* to consider a problem and do something about it "Jesse should face the fact that he's an alcoholic."

6. **nursery school** *n.* a school that cares for very young children "Marissa leaves her son at a nursery school on the way to work."

7. **on the other hand** *idiom* but "I'm very tired and want to go to bed. On the other hand, I have a lot of work to do."

8. **relative** *n.* a member of one's family; a person related to one by blood or marriage "Most of Ping's relatives live in China."

9. **successful** *adj.* having done well "Lenny is a successful coach; his teams are always good."

10. **suffer** *v.* to be damaged; to be hurt "If we don't work hard, our business will suffer."

11. **while** *conj.* during the time that "Roberta likes to listen to the radio while she's doing her homework."

PREVIEW QUESTIONS

Discuss these questions before reading the story.

1. A job gives a person money. What else does a job give us? For example, it gives us an opportunity to make new friends.
2. Is it easy to get good day care for young children? Explain your answer.
3. Do you think most husbands understand how much work goes into taking care of a home and young children? Explain your answer.

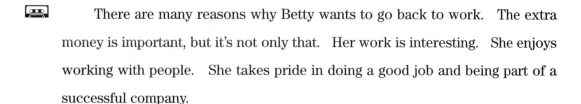 There are many reasons why Betty wants to go back to work. The extra money is important, but it's not only that. Her work is interesting. She enjoys working with people. She takes pride in doing a good job and being part of a successful company.

On the other hand, Betty is concerned about Michelle and Brian. Michelle is only three. There are no relatives who can care for Michelle while Betty is at work, or for Brian when he comes home from school. Betty's parents live 300 miles away. Jim's mother isn't well, and his father is dead.

Betty and Jim can pay someone to come to their house and take care of Michelle during the day and Brian after school. They can also send Michelle to a nursery school and Brian to an after-school center. However, Betty doesn't like the idea of having other people take care of her children. "There is no one like a mother to care for small children," she says. "Will our children suffer if I return to work?" she asks herself.

Last night, Betty and Jim talked about the situation for over an hour. It's fine with Jim if Betty goes back to work. It's also fine with him if she decides to stay home to take care of the children. Betty's former boss is going to phone her tomorrow. She has to decide by then. She faces a tough decision. She doesn't know what to do. What advice would you give her?

COMPREHENSION

Answer these questions in pairs or small groups. Use your own ideas to answer questions with an asterisk.

1. What does Betty enjoy?
2. In what does she take pride?
3. Why can't Betty's parents care for Michelle and Brian?
4. Why can't Jim's parents?
5. Why doesn't Betty like the idea of having other people care for her children?
*6. Do you think her children will suffer if she returns to work?
7. How does Jim feel about her returning to work?
*8. Do you think Betty will go back to work or stay home? Explain your answer.

STORY COMPLETION

Pains in Her Stomach

My sister is a very good lawyer and loves her work, but I'm worried about her health. She has pains in her stomach but won't see a doctor, and I can't force her to go.

away	on the other hand	concerned	face
advice	successful	situation	pride

My sister is married, has two lovely children, and is a _____ lawyer. She takes great _____ in her work and family, but I'm _____ about her health. She has pains in her stomach, and they won't go _____.

My sister, however, doesn't want to _____ her problem and won't listen to my _____ to see a doctor.

It's a difficult _____. I know she should see a doctor. _____, I can't force her to go.

SHARING INFORMATION

Discuss these questions in pairs or small groups. Space is provided to write your answers if you wish.

1. What do you think is the main reason most people work? Is it for the money, or because they enjoy their work and take pride in it?

    _____

    _____

2. Do you think most men would feel uncomfortable to have their wives earn more money than they do? Explain your answer.

    _____

    _____

3. Do you think that a day-care center, or another adult, can provide child care that is almost the same as a mother's? Explain your answer.

    _____

    _____

4. Even mothers who stay home often send their preschool children to a nursery school for part of the day. Why?

    _____

    _____

5. If a married woman works outside the home, do you think that the husband and wife should share equally in doing the housework? Explain your answer.

    _____

    _____

6. Is that what usually happens?

    _____

    _____

7. Do men in the United States often share in the cooking, doing the dishes, and other kinds of housework?

    _____

    _____

8. Do men in your country often share in the cooking, doing the dishes, and other kinds of housework?

    _____

    _____

SYNONYMS

Synonyms are words that have the same or a similar meaning. In the blank spaces, write a synonym for the underlined word or words.

injured	extremely	concerned	be polite	while
cop	deserve	position	realize	approach

1. Audrey has a very good <u>job</u> at the bank. _____
2. It's important to <u>have good manners</u>. _____
3. A <u>police officer</u> is directing traffic. _____
4. <u>During the time that</u> Gino was driving home, he was thinking about his girlfriend. _____
5. I'm <u>very</u> busy preparing for tomorrow's meeting. _____
6. Our business is losing money. We have to change our <u>way of doing things</u>. _____
7. You <u>should get</u> an A in math. _____
8. I didn't <u>know</u> that you and Bobby were cousins. _____
9. Sharon <u>hurt</u> her leg. _____
10. I'm <u>worried</u> about these bills. _____

ANTONYMS

Antonyms are words that have opposite meanings. In the blank spaces, write an antonym for each word.

take care of	start	away	sick	slow down
old-fashioned	cheerful	stay	in favor of	complicated

1. sad _____
2. go faster _____
3. opposed to _____
4. neglect _____
5. here _____
6. simple _____
7. modern _____
8. well _____
9. finish _____
10. leave _____

A

absolutely adv. 10
accurate adj. 160
ad (advertisement) n. 102
admit v. 80
adore v. 150
advice n. 172
afford v. 128
ago adv. 6
agree v. 128
allow v. 62
a lot of idiom 2
already adv. 120
although conj. 102
ambitious adj. 58
angry adj. 32
animal shelter n. 68
annoy v. 80
anymore adv. 2
appendicitis n. 54
appendix n. 54
appetite n. 36
apply v. 106
approach n. 164
argue v. 116
around adv. 6
article n. 84
as . . . as conj. 112
as soon as conj. 18
at first idiom 102
at least idiom 32
at least idiom 90
at once idiom 54
attractive adj. 14
away adv. 172
awful adj. 54
ax n. 72

B

bank account n. 106
bargain n. 128
bark v. 80
bay n. 142
beach n. 142
beautician n. 106
beauty salon n. 106

be back idiom 28
beer n. 46
be in favor of idiom 164
believe v. 18
belong v. 68
benefit n. 40
BENGAY® n. 50
besides adv. 14
bet v. 40
Big Mac® n. 2
biography n. 98
bite v. 80
bleed v. 150
bookkeeper n. 84
boring adj. 80
borrow v. 138
both pronoun 128
bowling n. 14
brake n. 138
break n. 6
breathing n. 58
bribe n. 128
briefcase n. 112
bright adj. 14
business administration n. 80
by the way idiom 160

C

calm v. 24
calm adj. 62
calm down v. 128
calorie n. 2
can n. 24
captain n. 80
cardiologist n. 62
cashier n. 102
catch v. 90
certainly adv. 2
charge v. 68
cheerful adj. 168
cherry n. 72
chop down v. 72
close call idiom 164
coin n. 142
come on idiom 68
come on idiom 134

complain v. 32
complaint n. 124
complicated adj. 164
concerned (about) adj. 172
condition n. 62
cooperate v. 36
cop n. 156
coronary adj. 62
count on idiom 40
couple n. 14
couple (of) n. 76
crazy adj. 90
crazy about idiom 10
credit n. 164
crowded adj. 58
curious adj. 168
cushion n. 120
customer n. 106

D

damage v. 128
damage n. 150
dangerous adj. 84
darling n. 10
date v. 150
deaf adj. 160
deal n. 120
deal with v. 164
decaffeinated (decaf) adj. 28
decision n. 172
degree n. 146
demanding adj. 32
deny v. 50
deserve v. 164
dessert n. 28
diamond n. 18
diet n. 2
diploma n. 106
disappear v. 18
disco n. 150
dressing n. 28
drive crazy idiom 84
drunk adj. 18
due adj. 98
due adj. 124
dumb adj. 146

E

efficient *adj.* 168
either *adv.* 116
else *adv.* 28
emergency *n.* 54
employment agency *n.* 102
empty *adj.* 128
encourage *v.* 146
engagement *n.* 18
engineering *n.* 168
enough *adj.* 50
especially *adv.* 6
even *adv.* 168
except (for) *prep.* 146
excited *adj.* 120
exciting *adj.* 142
expensive *adj.* 134
experience *n.* 102
explain *v.* 10
exterminator *n.* 124
extremely *adv.* 160

F

face *v.* 172
fail *v.* 98
fall apart *idiom* 138
fan *n.* 40
far *adv.* 106
favorite *n.* 14
fee *n.* 128
feed *v.* 68
feeling *n.* 6
fever *n.* 24
few *adj.* 28
fill out *v.* 102
fit *v.* 84
flash *v.* 156
flatter *v.* 134
foolish *adj.* 18
forever *adv.* 10
form *n.* 102
former *adj.* 168
fortunately *adv.* 62
freeze *v.* 142
French fries *n.* 2
fresh *adj.* 80

from time to time *idiom* 18
fun *n.* 72

G

gain *v.* 36
gamble *v.* 40
gee *idiom* 98
gee whiz *idiom* 72
gentle *adj.* 62
get *v.* 2
get along (with) *idiom* 40
get back *v.* 128
get into *v.* 168
get rid of *idiom* 124
give up *v.* 142
go ahead *idiom* 134
goal *n.* 98
go shopping *v.* 6
government *n.* 106
grade *n.* 80
grant *n.* 106
grow *v.* 106
guess *v.* 46
gymnastics *n.* 40

H

had better *idiom* 112
handle *v.* 58
handsome *adj.* 14
hard *adv.* 32
hardly *adv.* 54
hate *v.* 84
have got to *idiom* 46
have to *idiom* 6
head (heads) *n.* 142
head *v.* 142
heart attack *n.* 62
heartbroken *adj.* 76
hectic *adj.* 58
hesitate *v.* 14
hey *idiom* 120
hint *n.* 94
historic *adj.* 84
horrible *adj.* 116
how *adv.* 54
how *adv.* 72

How about ...? *idiom* 24
however *conj.* 14
hug *n.* 62
hurry *n.* 94

I

ignition *n.* 120
imagine *v.* 94
improve *v.* 124
in addition *idiom* 128
in advance *idiom* 128
injure *v.* 168
insurance *n.* 40
interest *n. & v.* 146
interview *n.* 106
in time *idiom* 150

J

jog *v.* 40
joke *n.* 76
joy *n.* 146
junk *n.* 84
just *adv.* 10
just *adv.* 84

K

keep *v.* 6
kid *v.* 24
kid *n.* 72
kill *v.* 50
kind *adj.* 10
kind *n.* 68

L

lack *n.* 124
license *n.* 106
license *n.* 160
lie *n.* 72
lie *v.* 72
lie down *v.* 24
like *prep.* 32
live up to *idiom* 146
loaf (of bread) *n.* 28
lonely *adj.* 18
lose *v.* 2

lottery *n.* 40
loud *adj.* 160
loyal *adj.* 68
luck *n.* 2

M

ma'am (madam) *n.* 94
madly in love *idiom* 14
main *adj.* 98
major *adj.* 58
mall *n.* 68
manager *n.* 58
mark *n.* 98
mean *adj.* 134
merengue *n.* 6
midnight *n.* 150
miss *v.* 40
miss *v.* 102
motivate *v.* 146
mousetrap *n.* 116

N

nag *v.* 84
neat *adj.* 84
neighborhood *n.* 124
neither *adj.* 146
noon *n.* 84
normal *adj.* 76
not . . . at all *idiom* 146
nursery school *n.* 172

O

obviously *adv.* 150
of course *idiom* 10
off duty *idiom* 168
officer *n.* 156
old-fashioned *adj.* 18
on duty *idiom* 146
only *adj.* 14
on the other hand *idiom* 172
operate *v.* 102
opposite *n.* 84
oral *adj.* 98
overweight *adj.* 58
own *adj.* 14
own *v.* 36

oxygen *n.* 62

P

pace *n.* 58
pack *n.* 58
pack rat *n.* 84
pain *n.* 46
paperwork *n.* 168
parrot *n.* 164
pass *v.* 106
passenger *n.* 84
patience *n.* 134
patient *adj.* 28
patient *n.* 54
pay *n.* 32
pension *n.* 40
permit *n.* 134
personnel *n.* 168
pet *n.* 68
pick up *v.* 6
plant *v.* 72
pleasant *adj.* 36
plenty (of) *adj.* 50
polite *adj.* 164
position *n.* 168
pound *n.* 2
pregnant *adj.* 124
pretty *adv.* 40
pride *n.* 146
promise *v.* 18
pronounce *v.* 90
pronunciation *n.* 90
proud (of) *adj.* 164
pull over *v.* 156
puppy *n.* 68

Q

quart *n.* 28
quickly *adv.* 102
quit *v.* 146
quite *adv.* 36

R

race *v.* 146
racetrack *n.* 40
radar *n.* 160

rapid *adj.* 58
rarely *adv.* 36
react *v.* 18
realize *v.* 160
really *adv.* 128
reason *n.* 168
registration *n.* 160
regular *adj.* 28
relative *n.* 172
relax *v.* 46
reliable *adj.* 40
rent *n.* 124
require *v.* 102
rest *n.* 138
right away *idiom* 46
right now *idiom* 46
roach (cockroach) *n.* 124
route *n.* 84
rub *v.* 50
rush *v.* 84

S

security deposit *n.* 128
seem *v.* 14
selfish *adj.* 142
senior *n.* 80
service station *n.* 138
set *adj.* 18
set *v.* 116
several *adj.* 90
severe *adj.* 58
sewing machine *n.* 102
shake *n.* 2
should *v.* 24
shy *adj.* 14
silly *adj.* 10
siren *n.* 156
situation *n.* 18
slam *v.* 150
slap *n.* 76
slap in the face *idiom* 76
slave *n.* 32
slice *n.* 58
slippery *adj.* 84
slow down *v.* 150
so *adv.* 10

so *adv.* 14
so *conj.* 32
so *conj.* 120
soccer *n.* 80
social worker *n.* 14
sort *n.* 84
sound *v.* 28
So what? *idiom* 116
special *adj.* 6
spoil *v.* 50
sports car *n.* 146
spot *n.* 50
stand *v.* 120
starve *v.* 2
step *n.* 10
still *adv.* 36
stitch *n.* 150
stranger *n.* 80
stroke *n.* 160
stupid *adj.* 72
subject *n.* 80
successful *adj.* 172
such *adv.* 10
such *adj.* 124
suddenly *adv.* 150
suffer *v.* 172
summary *n.* 98
super (superintendent) *n.* 128
sure *adv.* 6
sympathetic *adj.* 146

T

tail *n.* 80
tail (tails) *n.* 142
take it easy *idiom* 32
terrier *n.* 68
terrific *adj.* 134
threaten *v.* 146
throw out *v.* 84
ticket *n.* 156
tiny *adj.* 124
tip *n.* 94
tire *n.* 138
together *adv.* 14
too *adv.* 6

toss *v.* 142
tough *adj.* 94
traffic light *n.* 160
train *v.* 68
training *n.* 106
treat *v.* 32
treat *v.* 62
trouble *n.* 46
trust *v.* 18
truth *n.* 72
tuition *n.* 106
turn *n.* 32
twice *adv.* 40

U

unemployment compensation *n.* 102
unit *n.* 62
upset *adj.* 24
used to *idiom* 156

V

view *n.* 18

W

wag *v.* 80
warn *v.* 18
waste *n.* 138
way *n.* 50
weakness *n.* 40
wear *v.* 150
What's the matter? *idiom* 46
while *n.* 124
while *conj.* 172
wild *adj.* 146
women's lib
  (women's liberation) *n.* 164
wonder *v.* 18
wonder *n.* 90
wonderful *adj.* 10
workaholic *n.* 58
worry *v.* 6
worse *adj.* 58
wrestler *n.* 98
wrong *adj.* 32

Y

yard *n.* 72
yellow pages *n.* 106